Unity and Diversity
in World's Living Religions

A Compact Survey

Unity and Diversity in World's Living Religions

A Compact Survey

Muhammad Hedayetullah

*Our mission is to efficiently provide the world's finest, most comprehensive book publishing
service, enabling every author to experience success. To find out how to publish your
book, your way, and have it available worldwide, visit us online at www.trafford.com*

Trafford rev. 11/12/2010

 www.trafford.com

North America & International
toll-free: 1 888 232 4444 (USA & Canada)
phone: 250 383 6864 ♦ fax: 812 355 4082

To MY BELOVED WIFE

AL-HAJJ FARIDUNNAHAR

TABLE OF CONTENTS

FOREWORD

Dr. Muhammad Hedayetullah's concise and concentrated study of the world's religions is a timely addition to the vast amount of books and articles on this subject which the non-academic reader has no time or preparation to study and absorb. All too often, texts are targeted to a particular audience and not to those who may be seeking a general and broader access to basic knowledge about the major faiths currently in existence. This is why the present volume meets such a need admirably; it is neither pedantic nor superficial. Drawing upon his lifetime of learning and teaching, Dr. Hedayetullah has composed a compact survey of the world's living religions which highlights in a few swift strokes the essential diversity and the unity of these spiritual movements that have shaped the world we live in, for better or for worse.

Dr. Hedayetullah's book will come as a welcome and easily accessible introduction to those wishing to take a "crash course", so to say, in the major religions in order to gain insight into their birth, growth and present status. For some readers, this hors d'œuvre will be sufficient; for others, it will be what their appetite for further reading and exploration. In both cases, this little volume will have accomplished its task: to have introduced the curious beginner to the vast field of Comparative Religion. Professor Hedayetullah is no stranger to this terrain; he has toiled in it all of his life and knows more than he could express in this book because of its limited scope and succinct aim. For those readers wishing to know more about Islam, it is strongly recommended that they consult his other previous books on this subject.

May the volume you now hold in your hands be the beginning of an exciting and stimulating faith journey that engages both your intellect and heart.

Dr. Angelika Maeser Lemieux
September 16, 2010
St. Laurent, Quebec

ABOUT THE AUTHOR

Dr. Muhammad Hedayetullah has a dynamic academic background: as a student, he first attended the Arabic-Islamic institution, Madrasah-i-ʿAlia, Dhaka, Bangladesh, whence he obtained his first Master degree in *hadith* (Islamic Tradition--M.M.); then switching to the English education system, he obtained B.A. (Honours) and a 2nd Masters degree in Islamic History and Culture from Dhaka University.

With a Ford Foundation scholarship, he studied at the Institute of Islamic Studies, McGill University, whence he obtained his 3rd Masters degree in Islamic Studies. Then moving to Hamilton, he studied at McMaster University and obtained his Ph.D. in Comparative Religion.

The author has a teaching career of about 38 years beginning in different colleges in Bangladesh as a Lecturer of Islamic History and Culture. Before coming to Canada, he was a Research Associate at the Institute of Islamic Research, Karachi, Pakistan. As a Teaching Assistant, he taught Comparative Religion at McMaster University. He was a Lecturer of Islamic Studies at Lancaster University, England. Back in Canada, he joined as a Research Fellow at the Institute of Islamic Studies, McGill University. Finally, he taught for 25 years at Vanier College, Montreal, as a Professor of Humanities and Comparative Religion.

To his credit, there are some books and articles published in scholarly journals. His last book entitled: <u>Muslim-Christian/East-West Relations Up To The Fall Of Baghdad</u>, was published in 2007.

Dr. Muhammad Hedayetullah may be reached at his e-mail address **hedayet_kutir@yahoo.com** and via **telephone/fax at (514) 747-6695**. You can also visit his Face Book page at **www.facebook.com/muhammad.hedayetullah**.

ACKNOWLEDGEMENTS

I wish to thank the individuals who inspired me to write this book. Foremost, I must mention the names of my beloved wife, Al-Hajj Faridunnahar, who inspired me to write this book; my son, Fuad, whose practical help, in particular, facilitated my work in writing this book. Finally, my friend and brother-like Mohammed Ibrahim, who gave me his helping hand in finishing the work of this book. The next persons whose well-wishes also inspired me to write this book are my daughter, Nishat Sultana and her husband, Dr. Navid Zargeri and my two lovely grand-daughters, Safa and Shadi Zargeri. Apart from the members of my family, the person who spent her valuable time reading and reviewing the manuscript is my friend and colleague, Dr. Angelika Maeser Lemieux.

ABSTRACT

Since Comparative Religion or World Religion is the major field of my study, I have been planning for sometime to write a book on this subject, but in order to keep it to a reasonable length , I have decided to focus upon the living religions of the world; to further this plan, one of my colleagues, Dr. Angelika Maser Lemieux inspired me and gave me a helping hand.

At the outset, it should be noted that religions of all geographical areas and cultures are basically one, and the Ultimate Reality is also One; the only difference is the name by which the ultimate Reality is identified and worshipped by different peoples of the world. It should also be stated that there has never been a community without a "religion" notwithstanding the way of worshipping; for example, Papua New Guinea, is probably the last human settlement on the south-east end of the Pacific Ocean which was visited by Pope John Paul II during the last days of his papacy. Moreover, despite the great variety and diversity of religious expression spread over geographical space and historical eras, there is an underlying unity of purpose which can be discerned.

This work deals with all the living religions of the world on the basis of non-Semitic and Semitic—East and West respectively. Hinduism of India is the oldest non-Semitic religion of the world—beginning at least from 1500 B.C. with a large number of deities followed by Buddhism, Jainism, Sikhism and Zoroastrianism. The next country is China with three religions: Buddhism, Confucianism and Taoism; and the final eastern country is Japan with two religious systems, Shintoism and Buddhism.

Next, this book surveys the three Semitic religions--Judaism, Christianity and Islam—beginning with Moses in 1200 B. C. with the Torah, then Jesus with Injil (The Old and the New Testaments respectively), David with Jabbur (Psalms) and finally Muhammad with the Qur'an.

Semitic religions are well-known for their comprehensive subject-matter—socio-religious, ethical and moral. They particularly emphasized the significance of rituals in order to show the relevance of rituals to the worshippers' lives—this-worldly as well as spiritual.

PREFACE

At the outset, it should be stated that basically religion is one, and so is the Ultimate Reality or the divinity; the only difference is in names and the ways of performing worship. Thus, religions are different paths to salvation.

Religion is a large and complex phenomenon. Religious experience is definable as an experience of "ultimate valuations", "as the relationship between man and the superhuman power he believes in and feels himself to be dependent on"(1). According to Jakob Burckhardt, "Religions are the expression of the eternal and indestructible metaphysical craving of human nature. Their grandeur is that they represent the whole super-sensual complement of man, all that he cannot himself provide"(2).

We also know that the theme of religion is "redemption" or protection from the unseen powers that hinder man from communing with God. According to Friedrich Schleiermacher, "the feeling of absolute dependence" is an important part of religion. However, Hegel does not agree with this "feeling" and said that if this is the condition then "dogs would be the best Christians, for dogs exhibit this feeling to perfection."(3). However, St. Augustine defined the word religion as "finding again of some thing that has been lost, while Lactantius saw it as a derivative of religare, "to tie". Therefore, religion means the "tie" or the idea of being tied to a higher or the highest "power". We may conclude the present subject by stating: "The impulse toward religion is an essential part of man's endowment. Religion manifests itself as a sum, of beliefs relating to a reality which is not provable by experience, but which is nevertheless an unconditional certainty to the believer. This reality represents an ultimate standard in the life of the believer and prompts him to certain modes of action"(4).

The primary object of religion is to answer man's fearful questions and to liberate him from the hindrances that interfere communication with the Ultimate Reality. That is to say, in religion humans face a power superior to them. Therefore, they seek to obtain the divine help whose protection they need against that "power". They long for peace and truth and want to achieve immortality.

From what has already been stated above, it is clear that there has never been and still there is no society without some form of religion. That is to say, religion has always occupied an important place in human life—society, history and philosophy. Presently, when the very existence of humanity is threatened by political and military conflicts, especially nuclear warfare, man appears to be puzzled without any fixed attachments to the values of the society save concerned solely in the present. In his concern about the very existence, he strives tirelessly for success—prosperity, happiness, etc. "But within his deepest self, he seeks a firm ground; he wishes to see some meaning to his existence. Men are filled with longings for peace and for redemption."(5).

THE PREANIMISTIC THEORY

The theory of religious evolution was questioned by Taylor's pupils, R. R. Marett and Andrew Lang, as not according with the facts. At the primitive stage, mythologies dealing with gods can be shown to have existed side by side with belief in departed souls and animate nature. There were peoples who did not believe in spirits or souls. "According to Marett, the origin of religion must be sought in the dynamistic conception of a general impersonal power which manifests itself in unusual phenomena and can cause extraordinary effects (belief in mana).The power so experienced can be conceived as an active will. Along with this primeval experience,…, goes the instinct that dangerous powers (negative <u>mana</u>) must be fended off (idea of taboo")(6).

THE THEORY OF ORIGINAL MONOTHEISM

This theory was derived from observations by Andrew Lang who demonstrated that the concept of high gods in the sky was at first promoted by ancient Australian tribes. "The theory was systematically worked out by the Jesuit father Wilhelm Schmidt (<u>Der Ursprung der Gottesidee</u>, 12 vols., 1912-1955) and his culturo-historical school of ethnology"(7). The author further states that "At the beginning of all religious development…stood the belief in an omnipotent supreme being.…" (8) In the course of cultural and historical degeneration, later peoples lost this belief and instead developed a harsher mythology of polytheism and spirits. (9) That is to say, people with increasing cultural development, felt the need for special deities as aids in their diverse lifestyle. This stage was followed by the coming of Jesus Christ who taught people to believe in the "Heavenly Father once more"(10).

We may conclude the present subject by stating that "… belief in a supreme being had been an essential component of the oldest cultures, for among Australians, Polynesians, Zulus, Bushmen, Congo tribes, and Mongolians can be demonstrated the worship of a 'Primal Father'"(11). Thus, the evolution from monotheism to polytheism developed "because man, with increasing culture, felt the need for special deities as aids in his manifold enterprises." (12)

The primitive circumstances under which religion began with a belief in spirits, powers, magic and fetishes, and with sacrifices to images of divinities, showed that early man realized that his dependence on an unknown power arouses hopes and love as well as fear. To demonstrate his relationship with divinity, man performs prayer, sacrifice and other rituals. Some individuals in the religious life of man, such as prophet, founders, mystics, priests and reformers develop particular features or characters in religion which resulted in so-called "different religions".

The concept of religion encircles the whole vast sphere from belief in objects soaked thoroughly with mana to selfless dedication to a personal deity. Different and sometime contradictory answers are given to the question of the type of miraculous or supernatural power. Branches of religion are as many as are the names of the deities to whom people have been praying and making sacrifices; but all share some aspects, such as moral requirement, rituals , hopes of judgment and redemption.

Our next issue is the ultimate concerns of religion: ultimate concerns or values presuppose several identifying characteristics.

The first is that an ultimate concern has priority in the system of concerns which institutes a personality or culture. From this, it follows that an ultimate concern has the function of giving meaning, purpose and direction to human life. An ultimate concern is one to which in a crisis a person willingly sacrifices every other valuable things, including life itself. Historically it may be observed that such concerns or values tend to take on religious significance, whether officially leveled religious or not.

Religious aspect of human experience is to imagine a straight line along which are placed a person's concerns. At the other end, are ultimate concerns. "As one moves along this line from the superficial to the serious concerns, one observes the increasing emergence of religious quality. Also, if the latter end of the line represents what has been called *ultimate concern*, then one may perhaps call the interests near this end *penultimate*, or possessing an almost religious quality."(13).

HOLINESS

Another feature of "ultimate concerns is their emotive or affective accompaniment;" viz, the holy. "Like religion, the terms holy and sacred" are generally used with different meanings. Here it is easy to begin with Rudolph Otto's approach to the holy as an unparalleled or unique emotions.(14).

To Otto, the holy is an uncommon affection, for the good reason that it is the human response to transcendence, "or in theistic terms, to God".

"The holy is the affective accompaniment of ultimate concern and commitment". "A religion may thus be defined as an existent system of holy forms."(15) These forms are models or specimen of human attitudes, beliefs or practices; they are systematically organised ways of thinking, feeling or doing, both individual and social. But usually they are mixture of both.

HISTORY

Since old or early times, history has been playing an important role in the study of religion. By the way, "both the word and the discipline are Greek in origin". Greek and Roman historians sometimes dealt with religious beliefs and practices as part of their historical studies. "In the ancient Greco-Roman world, the stoics were preeminent for their interest in the diverse religious phenomena of their world."(16)

Since the early modern times historical study began, scholars put great emphasis on a "critical evaluation of the sources" whence historians collected their information. Modern study and writings have demonstrated a great emphasis and varieties. A significant concern was demonstrated with the history of religion. Primarily applied to Western religions, this study has stressed free and critical study of biblical and Christian sources, but the history of religions has since the nineteenth century also tried to include all religions of the world. However, it has been particularly concerned with the critical rearrangement or reconstruction (as well as the communication to Occidental readers) of important aspects of the different Oriental religions. Thus, it also has created a constant interest in the comparative study of the world's religions, and these historical forms of study are still continuing.

<u>TYPES OF RELIGION</u>

At the outset, it should be mentioned that religious experience demands and receives symbolic expression for itself. In any specific situation, this symbolic expression involves some altogether definite, particular symbols, around which gathers a group of individuals who express their final concern through them. By some such process, an actual religion or religious order (real religion) comes into being. In other words, "a religion comes into being and maintains itself as a community centering in some concrete symbol or symbol system for the expression of ultimate value"(17).

The next question is "what are the world's living religions"? In this connection, we propose to consider the oldest one and the ones following that one of the same region—East and West. Accordingly, we propose to begin with the eastern or non-Semitic religions: Hinduism, Jainism, Buddhism; Chinese and Japanese religions followed by the Western or Semitic religions of the West, namely, Judaism, Christianity and Islam.

It may be added that the first type usually has a plurality of religious objects or divinity; that is to say, it is polytheistic. Its many divinities are located within the common world of nature and society and usually personified statements of the human religion to this world or to particular aspect of it. This kind of religion has sometimes been identified as "nature-culture religion" as well as cosmic religion. This type of religion considers the world itself as divine.(18).

The second type of religion finds the religious object away from the secular world of nature and society. Here the religious object is usually conceived as singular—a deity. This kind of religion represents the achievement by the human mind of what is called an Archimedean point outside the world. Often this type of religion is classified as transcendental monism. It may also be called acosmaic religion. The best example of this type of religion is "Jainism and philosophic Hinduism."(19). Popular

Hinduism undoubtedly is known as a religion of the first rather than of the second type.

The third type of religion believes in religious objects both within the practical or physical world and beyond. It believes in a transcendental or super-natural Being under whose command runs the whole universe. The basic concern of this type of religion is with one God, well-known as <u>monotheism</u>. With the second type, it shares a transcendent point beyond the common world. "Yet with the first type it asserts the reality and goodness of the world of nature and culture. These features taken together generate what has been called a <u>linear view</u> of history, in contrast to the cyclic view of the first two types. Hence this third type is often identified as <u>historical relgion</u>"(20).

The basic interest of this type of religion is with one God: hence it is called <u>monotheism</u>. Therefore, the monotheistic religions of mankind are "Judaism, Christianity, Islam, Zoroastrianism, and possibly Sikhism"(21).

PHILOSOPHY OF RELIGION

Philosophy in its numerous aspects is concerned with the study of religion or the world's faiths. This phenomenon is present in all religious traditions such as Indian, Chinese, Greek and Christian. The source of these varieties of religious thought lies in the human being's quest for meaning and values: his ultimate concern. Thus, "in tracing the implication and bearings of the religious experience, people have been led to concepts of an altogether inclusive totality; and this is a type of thinking that constitutes the distinctive feature of philosophy"(22). For example, in ancient Greece, critical thinking upon religious mythology was a primary source of philosophical study. Since Kant (1724—1804) and Hegel (1770—1831), "philosophy of religion has been the customary label for a philosophic approach to religious issues and problems"(23). Thus the philosophic explanation of and information about religious matters continue to be major issues and methods of study of religious issues. Often in the present situation the term philosophical theology is applied to this kind of study.

. Thus, "In tracing the implications and bearings of the religious experience, people have been led to concepts of an altogether inclusive totality; and this is a type of thinking that constitutes the distinctive feature of philosophy"(24).

MYSTICISM

Mysticism is another facet of religion. It permeates the major religions, yet there are few subjects which are liable to so many different and conflicting usages than mystic and mysticism. The adjective mystical may be applied widely but reasonably to any form of religious experience in which "cognition" is emphasized.

Interestingly, the above definition conflicts with the current popular misunderstanding to the effect that mystical means irrational which means that reason and mysticism are mutually exclusive. From the definition given here, it may be concluded that "intuitive forms or qualities of knowing vary independently with rationality. Some mystical states are clearly irrational and stoutly resist attempts at rational checking or testing. Others appear to be quite the opposite"(25).

Generally, the term has been applied to two different types of experience: one of these is often called <u>mysticism of communion</u>, and the other is named <u>mysticism of ontological union or absorption</u>. It is well-known that mystics speak habitually of <u>union</u> with the religious object so that all separate identity disappears in eternal union with the Ultimate Reality(God). Secondly , the mysticism of "absorption" has very often had the additional involvement of hinting at a separate philosophic outlook. For example, Aldous Huxley once wrote of this outlook as the "perennial philosophy" happening again and again in many "times and places" (26).

ENDNOTES - PREFACE

1. Schoeps, Hans-Joachim. <u>The Religions of Mankind</u>: <u>Their Origin and Development.</u> Translated from the German by Richard and Clara Winston. New York: Doubleday & Company, Inc., 1968, p. 12.

2. <u>Ibid</u>.

3. Ibid.

4. <u>Ibid</u>., p. 3.

5. <u>Ibid</u>., p. v.

6. <u>Ibid</u>., p. 7.

7. <u>Ibid</u>., p. 8.

8. <u>Ibid</u>.

9. <u>Ibid</u>.

10. <u>Ibid</u>.

11. Hutchison, John A.. <u>Paths of Faith</u>. Montreal: McGraw-Hill Book Company, 1969, p. 5.

12. Schoeps, <u>op. cit</u>., p. 8.

13. Cf. Tillich, P. <u>The Protestant Era</u>. Chicago: University of Chicago Press; Perry, R. B. <u>General Theory of Value. London:</u> Longmans, 1926, 115f; Otto, R. <u>The Idea of the Holy</u>.

London: Oxford University Press, 1923, ref. in Hutchison, op. cit., p. 6, also cf. Schoeps, op. cit., p.1.

14. Cf. Otto, op. cit.,

15. Hutchison, op. cit., p. 7.

16. Ibid., p. 12.

17. Ibid., p. 14.

18. Eliade, Mircea. Cosmos and History. New York: Harper, 1953, ref. in Hutchison, op. cit., p. 14.

19. Hutchison, op. cit., p. 15.

20. Ibid.

21. Ibid.

22. Hutchison, op. cit., p. 19.

23. Ibid., p. 11.

24. Ibid., p. 19.

25. Ibid.

26. Aldous Huxley. The Perennial Philosophy. New York: Harper, 1945, ref. Hutchison, op. cit., p. 20.

CH. 1: INDIAN RELIGIONS

(A) <u>Hinduism</u>

In English, the title <u>Hinduism</u> was first used in 1829.(1) Eastern religions have been called "Religions of eternal cosmic law" because they start with immutable laws of being. "They manage entirely without notion of a personal God, or predict a completely different view of salvation and loss of salvation than do the religions based upon the Bible [and the Qur'an] (2) In other words, fundamental ideas put them dramatically opposed to the Semitic Religions. (By the way, the word Hinduism comes from Hindustan, the Persian name given by the Muslim rulers of India--711-1858 C.E.) It should be stated here that Hinduism is also known as Brahmanism—the term Brahmanism comes from the Hindu priestly caste of Brahmans, not from the god Brahman (Brahma).

Hinduism, the oldest religion of the world (between 1500 and 800 B.C.), is based on the Veda (knowledge), not a revealed scripture but a collection and compilation of Indian (Hindu) sages' inspired words in Sanskrit. It is basically a sacrificial religion with a number of gods (as many as 365 in legendary counts) and a "pluralistic cosmology".

The Veda is divided into four parts: (1) Rig-Veda (knowledge of hymns). In eloquent and powerful words, the gods, especially the king of gods, Indra, are called to participate in the sacrificial meal. The rhymes reveal a good deal about the Aryan tribes who migrated from Central Asia into India around 1800 B.C. (2) Samaveda (chants) presents the major melodies with which the singing priests accompany the sacrifices (3) Yajurveda (science of sacrificial formulas) is a summery of the formulas and prayers, that the priest must utter in low voice as he makes sacrifice. It is for this reason that the Yajurveda is considered a sort of liturgical book. (4) Atharvaveda (Veda of spells) contains spells and the exorcism Brahmans must use for different occasions.(3)

The philosophical and mystical Hindu scripture is, of course, the Upanishads (confidential sessions) contain esoteric wisdom of great value for priests and their disciples. They influenced even some Western philosophers like Schelling and Schopenhauer. These Upanishads are also called Vedanta (conclusion of the Vedas)—because they represent the final thoughts on the Vedic texts. "The mystical piety of Upanishads shifts the emphasis from knowledge of sacrificial techniques and their meaning to salvation through the liberating knowledge conferred by contemplation."(4) "The union of the human soul (Atman)", concludes the author, "with the world spirit (Brahman) becomes the goal of salvation."(5)

This goal is to be gained by insight: the famous formula: tat tawam asi (thou art that) expresses this identification. "Atman Brahman mysticism unites self and the universe, that is salvation, which is achieved by a kind of miraculous illumination."(6)

(B) THE PURANAS

There is still another kind of religious literature which serves as a source of study for Hinduism, namely, the Puranas (ancient tales). There are eighteen Puranas in existence of which the best known are the (1) Bhagavata, (2) Vayu, (3) Vishnu and (4) Agni. Their subject-matter is a mixture of tales, teaching and general matters. Usually Puranas deal with matters like (1) creation of the universe, (2) re-creation of the universe, (3) pedigree of gods and sages, (4) ages of the world rulers and (5) genealogies of kings. Although the Puranas are not as important as other works of Indian religion, as mentioned above, their importance as sources of popular piety cannot be minimised, for it is very great.

According to Hindu tradition, the four ends of human life are <u>Dharma</u>, <u>Artha</u>, <u>Kama</u> or <u>Karma</u> and <u>moksha</u>. In addition to the achievement of <u>moksha</u> by <u>sanyasin </u>(saint), and to its visualisation by philosophers and seers, traditional Indian society has also placed its highest social values upon those individuals who are said to have achieved this highest goal of freedom or release. Common Hindus, struggling in the middle of objects and illusions or deceptions of this world, may not enjoy or quickly anticipate this fulfillment for themselves, but they can praise those champions of the spirit who have done so. Compassionately, they can share in the achievement of others.

(C) <u>FOUR ENDS OF HUMAN LIFE</u>

It has already been mentioned that the main objective of human life, according to Hindu tradition, is to achieve <u>moksha</u> (release),that is "emancipation" from all "fetters" and. obstacles. Yet, with the passing of time, "other goals were added to from the traditional tetrad"(7). Hinduism claims that its objective is to offer something to everyone under all human conditions. The four ends of human life, according to Hinduism, help to fulfill this claim and together they provide opportunities and scope for all the different capacities of a person's life. According to Hindu tradition, the four ends of human life (purushartha) are duty or righteousness (dharma), material success (artha), love or pleasure (kama), and emancipation (moksha).(8).

(D) **Hindu Practices: Three Paths To Salvation**

The usual Hindu tendency to inclusiveness which brought into existence the four ends of human life has also created the three yogas (ways) or margas (roads). These roads of life may be distinguished as arrangements of thoughts, practices and feeling planned to achieve release for those who walk them. It is also important to take note that the three paths are not separate from one another, the religious life of many pious Hindus is a combinations of all three. The three paths are bhakti (personal devotion), karma (works) and jnana (knowledge).

(E) **The Bhagavadgita (The Gita)**

These texts are still accepted by orthodox Hindus as having the force of law, whereas they are rejected by reformers like Gautama Buddha and Mahavira. However, The Gita (The Song of the Adorable One), is respected by all Hindus. Basically rooted in Atman-Brahman mysticism, it is in several ways a unique expression of Hindu religious feeling. "Originally a part of the great family epic the Mahabharata, it was composed around 500 B.C., and represents human fate in general in the figure of the youthful hero Arjuna. Before the beginning of a great civil war and before the decisive battle, Arjuna on his war chariot holds converse with his charioteer, Krishna, who reveals himself to Arjuna as an avatar of the god Vishnu."(9)

(F) The Gods of Hinduism

It is stated before that Hinduism is not a revealed religion, but one that has developed by accretions without any set creeds and a definite way of salvation as in Semitic religion. Instead, it has established many forms and planes of religious life, including fetishism, animal cults (e.g. holy cow), polytheism, henotheism and pantheism, which all exist side by side. "Because of this contradictory coexistence of subtle and sublime with crude and primitive views and customs, it has been called an 'encyclopedia of all religions' "(10).

It should be mentioned here that in Hinduism there are no specific dogmas, tenets and notion; as a result, in this religion there is a great religious tolerance. There are many venerated objects and many paths to salvation. Naturally, there are numerous gods, as mentioned before. However, Vishnu and Shiva have become most famous of all, whereas many-headed Brahma, who is believed to have created the world, has gone down in importance and as a result, Hindus today generally regard him as an impersonal universal principle, a kind of world soul. "Shiva, the antagonist of the demons, is a terrible god whose cult is compounded of gloomily ascetic and wild, cruel and often orgiastic features". "As a fertility god", continues Schoeps, "his symbol is the phallus, his symbolic animal the bull."(11).

Among the more famous of goddesses are Durga, Kali (the Black), and Shakti—all of these belong to the type of magna mater, the Great Mother. "These three are cruel goddesses; temple paintings depict them with their mouths dripping blood."(12).

Interestingly, all these deities still have large followers, and yet there is no rivalry among these gods. The Indologist, Helmut von Glasenapp, has praised these Indian gods' position in contrast to the Europeans' in these words: "For the European, such juxtapositions would not work, because he associates the concept of God with certain ideas about divine characteristics or historical facts. The Hindu, on the other hand, sees in the various figures in his pantheon only more or less equal embodiments of an ultimate reality that bridges all contradictions."(13).

(G) <u>Doctrine of Karma</u>

What is the ultimate reality of Hinduism? It is the order of the whole universe, which is set by a single eternal law—<u>Karma</u>. "Karma is the Indian expression for belief in a moral order. The doctrine holds that every act performed in this life has moral significance and will influence the fate of the living being in subsequent incarnations. Consequently, all beings live under the conditions they have merited by their deeds."(14)

<u>Karma </u>is the accumulated result of every individual's each moment of existence on this earth. This theory of Karma as the path-finder of the ultimate goal goes back to the doctrine of "reincarnation" included in the Upanishads. Every Hindu tries by good deeds to assure himself a better "reincarnation in the next life"(15).

It should be stated that Hinduism recognises no end to existence. This is the reason why Hindus think historical events of only passing moment. That means, the wheel of <u>Samsara</u>—the cycle of rebirths—will never stop. All beings have immortal souls since all eternity, souls which merely change their material "husks" or outer covers. The direction of change is set forth in a proverb from the Upanishads: "As one does and as one goes, so one becomes. Whose acts are good becomes something good, whose acts are evil something evil."(16).

(H) <u>Hindu Caste System</u>

Undoubtedly, the caste system in Hinduism is an unprecedented phenomenon, especially in a religious system like Hinduism which is more or less quite open in all matters save the social. It is also well-known that the eternal cosmic law, accepted by all Hindus, finds its concrete expression in a steps of life which begins with plants and ends with the gods. From this universal law follow Hindu idea of caste on which the whole soci-religious system is based. H. von Glasenapp has defined the caste system as follows: "A caste is a group of persons who practice the same traditional occupation and are linked to one another by inherited rights, duties and customs. A person is born into this group, which takes care that its members marry only women of the same caste and eat only with persons of the same caste."(17).

The castes, as working classes, are organised in "corporations". Only the three highest, so-call "pure" castes have special rights and privileges. These are the (1) <u>Brahmins</u> (priests), (2) <u>Ksatrias</u> (warriors) and (3) <u>Vaishyas</u> (the working class).It should be stated here that the three upper castes, just mentioned, go through a special rite of "consecration" or purification called the "second birth", thus called "the twice born"(18).

However, the largest mass of the Hindus, who are responsible for the rest of the works of the society, popularly know as the "dirty or menial jobs" are marked as the Shudras. It must be emphasised here that for practical purposes, without their works, the nation could not maintain the hygienic aspect of it—the health matters, the physical well-being of the people. Unfortunately, those who are ritually unclean are declared "untouchables" or "Pariahs". "Persons who deal with unclean objects, such as laundrymen, or who kill living beings, such as fishermen or leather workers, stand lower than weavers and potters who practice less objectionable occupations"(19).

(I) **Hindu Reformers**

At this stage it is quite important to say a few words about Hindu reformers who considered their primary task is to demonstrate as precisely as possible to accommodate Hinduism to the post-classical religious atmosphere.

During the eighth and ninth centuries C. E., the philosopher Shankara Deva reinterpreted the Vedanta texts. His idea was that Brahman, the divine principle, is an impersonal unity found unconditional acceptance among learned Hindus. Shankara advanced the idea that different cults were nothing but equal ways to reach Brahma. "He divided knowledge into two categories, the lower takes the world for reality and the higher knowledge which sees the world as Maya (illusion) that distracts men from the solitude of the spirit." "The stage of higher knowledge", continues the author, "may be reached by study of the Veda and meditation, until at last the soul ascends to Brahma."(20).

About two centuries following Shankara, there appeared another reformer, named Ramanuja, who advocated a more personal concept of God (Brahma incarnated as Krishna). Ramanuja tried to lead men to contemplation of the God's good side to the "way of devotion" (<u>bhakti marga</u>) and personal love of God. In fact, Shankara and Ramanuja represent two alternative models of man's search for salvation, as Rudolf Otto once commented."(21)

At this point it should be stated unhesitatingly that the liberalism of Hinduism is unprecedented. For example, in modern India pantheists, henotheists, polytheists and even atheists along with orthodox Hindus live side by side in mutual understanding and respect. Apart from them, there are philosophical schools concerned with the operations of <u>Karma</u>. "Can man liberate himself from the fetters of <u>Samsara</u> of his own accord, by insight and knowledge, or does his salvation depend upon a helpful deity to whom he commands himself by worship and a good and merciful life? Hindus refer to these two schools of thought as monkey schools and cat schools because in one man clings to God like the monkey to its mother's neck, while in the other he is dependent on the deity, like the kitten that is carried in its mother's mouth."(22).

Thus redemption of the individual remains undecided, but Hinduism has no rule concerning a general salvation for the whole world. Because of the unlimited number of living beings, the wheel of <u>Samsara</u> will continue turning no matter how many "souls escape from the cycle of rebirths by attaining the state of bliss". Another important aspect of Hinduism is the fact that because of its lack of dogma, the Hindus find it easy to tolerate other religions.

We may conclude this discussion by saying that since the notion of prophecy is unknown to Hinduism, it gives more importance to religious obligations and social customs than to creeds and doctrines. And since Hinduism does not have any supreme authority who gives orders, almost everything in Hindu religious life is left to tradition and local usages.

(J) <u>Modern Hinduism</u>

Modern Hinduism has been boosted by the impulse from charismatic figures like Sri Ramakrishna (1834-1886), a visionary who freely preached the love of God, continued where Shankara had left, and accepted all religions as valid ways to salvation. Ramakrishna's ideas were put together in a number of folk sayings, such as "Different creeds are only different paths to the Almighty.... The avatar of (<u>sic</u>) saviour in different manifestations is the emissary of God. He resembles the viceroy of a mighty monarch. When disturbances break out in a remote province, the great prince sends a viceroy there to put the disturbance down. Thus God sends his (<u>sic</u>) avatar into the world whenever, anywhere in the world, religion is being crushed". "It is one and the same avatar who has plunged into the ocean of life and appears now as Krishna, now as Christ. Avatars—such as Rama, Krishna, Buddha, Christ—are related to the absolute Brahma as single waves to the whole ocean."(23). Mahatma Gandhi, Sri Aurobindo and Radhakrishnan, the great persons of modern India, are in the line of Ramakrishna.

At this point let us say a few words about the Mahatma Gandhi (1869-1948). It is well-known that Gandhi stands as contemporary India's greatest religio-political and social leader and the father of the free Indian nation by achieving India's independence from British rule in 1947. He was born and brought up in Gujarat in a Vaishya (merchant) family. He studied law in England, and after a brief return to India, lived for twenty years in South Africa as the leader of the Indian minority community there. During that time, his fundamental convictions and methods were formed, particularly of satyagraha ("truth force") or "the force which is born of truth and love". He turned the principle of ahimsa (originally used by Jainism) into a political weapon or philosophy in his fight for independence from British colonial rule. Nevertheless, he emphasised non-violence. Returning to India in 1915, he soon became the leader of the Indian National Congress. His leadership during three decades led to Indian independence..

Gandhi and the Gita: Speaking about the personal piety and spiritual significance of the Bhagavadgita , one wrier says: "... Bhagavadgita has won it many friends in the West (first translation 1785); and it has also enormously influenced countless Hindus. "As Gandhi," says Schoeps, "for example, declared: 'When disappointments confront me, I go to the Bhagavadgita, I read a verse here and a verse there, and in the midst of overwhelming tragedies I at once begin to smile." (24).

His struggle for the Parihas (social outcastes or untouchables) and for harmony between Hindus and Muslims led to his assassination in 1948.

Gandhi also represented Hinduism's claim to universality, especially against Christianity. One of Gandhi's high ranking political disciples was the first Prime Minister of an independent India (from the British colony) in 1947, Pandit Jawaharlal Nehru.

Sri Aurobindo Ghose (1872-1951) is remembered as the renewer of Yoga (cf. "Yoga" in <u>Encyclopaedia Britanica</u>). Aurobindo, too, was a world-known defender of the Indian National movement, even though in his thinking there was an influence of Christianity and Western ideas of progress and evaluation.

Next, the religious philosopher, Sarvepalli Radhakrishnan (1888-1958), in 1952 became the Vice President of the Independent Indian Republic and attempted to modernise the Vedanta (particularly the doctrines of Shankara) in order to bring Hinduism close to the West.

A more successful attempt to fulfill Radhakrishna's plan was made by Swami Vivekananda. In 1897, he founded the Ramakrishna Mission, with headquarters in Mombai, Kalikata and Madras, to spread the doctrines of the Vedanta, which gained a place in California. Fundamentally, its goal was a non-dogmatic union of all religions of the world; "Hinduism is regarded as mankind's eternal religion, from which non-Indians have drifted away either out of ignorance or deliberate apostasy" (25). It is reported that Vivekananda mentions a saying of Ramakrishnan : "I have tried all religions—Hinduism, Mohammedanism and Christianity—and I have found that all by different roads seek the same God" (26).In an attempt to further explain his understanding of the unity of all religions with a single ultimate goal, Ramakrishna is reported to have said that all religions—Indian and non-Indian are only "introductions to the universal, unitary vision of the Vedanta, the monistic conception of an all-embracing Oneness of all gods, living beings and things. By attaining the union of Atman and Brahman, the enlightened soul escapes from the eternal cycle of births"(27).

Before concluding the present subject, let us explain one important concept of Hinduism is dharma. The word dharma, which has been co-opted for the purpose in modern times, carries the original meaning of "righteous law", embracing both rite and ethics. Apart from this, modern India is country of many religions and many civilizations and thus in many ways without any resolution, specially in the matters of religion and practices. For example, the ban on the slaughter of cows results in many serious socio-political ills. The burning of widows, although forbidden by law, still continues. Many Sadhus (so-called holy men), who are actually crooks, kidnap babies to sacrifice to Kali or Durga. Monkeys are regarded as holy because the mythological monkey god Hanuman once helped Rama. The caste system does not facilitate any full-fledged social reform. However, notwithstanding often some unusual moral and social abuses, certain ethical rules are common to all Hindus.

(K) Mahavira and Jainism

In ancient India (also called the axis age, that is, approximately the seventh and sixth centuries B. C.), during which time, world-famous individuals such as Greek philosophers, Chinese thinkers like Lao-tzu and Confucius, and Mahavira and Buddha of India lived. Because of those figures, that age is known as the "ancient age of genius".

The urban revolution of that age had produced a sort of traditional civilization which has been maintaining its influence within the close circle of traditional society. It was a time of excitement and change around the world. What technical and social factors caused the change can only be investigated. Whatever the cause, out of the "axis ages" emerged new individuals, new ideas, thus a new direction for humanity.

In India, some have called this period the "age of the great heresies."(28). This is, of course, a wrong designation, since

Jainism and Buddhism, which came into being at this time, were not formally declared heresies. Later they were declared heresies for two reasons: they did not acknowledge the sacred authority of Vedas, and they rejected that touchstone of Hindu orthodoxy: caste.

We are told that in "India the axis age was a time of world-weariness and restiveness", when not only Buddha and Mahavira but a great many other people as well, shook the dust of society from their feet and sought the solitude of the forest, there to practice asceticism, to meditate, and, particularly to think new thoughts about human nature and human destiny.(29).

India produced a few teachers and bhaktas (mystics) of a quality of extraordinary teaching about the proper conduct of life and the goal of life. Each had a group of followers. Among teacher-devotees, Nataputta Vardhamana (the founder of Jainism), Gautama Buddha (of whom we will discus latter) and the anonymous seers of the Upanishads are renowned and have left long-lasting marks on India's thought and life.

However, despite the wide variety of doctrines, some patterns of similarity or unity do emerge. All these ancient teachers (save materialists and skeptics) acknowledged the emancipation or relief from mortality as the main goal of human beings. This goal was called <u>moksha</u> (salvation). Primarily, it pointed to a realism of salvation beyond all the limitations of the human related world. It is important to take note of that most of these teachers accepted the idea of <u>Karma</u> to achieve <u>Moksha</u> (salvation). The philosophic seers of the Upanishads extended the application of the <u>Karma</u> to many incarnations, past and future.

<u>Jainism: A Study of Extremism:</u> Among the old-time teachers, Nataputta Vardhamana, known as Mahavira, stands out for the extreme severity of his ascetic life and the clear, bold outlines of his philosophy. He was the first of a long line of Indian rebels against caste. He is more well-known as the founder of the religious community and tradition of Jainism. "Zimmer places Mahavira and Jainism as the first among those traditions of philosophy, art and religion which go back to the ancient pre-Aryan past of India, citing as evidence the realism and dualism of this philosophy in contrast to the Monistic idealism of the Aryan tradition, and pointing also to Jainism's own insistent tradition of a long line of twenty-four <u>tirthankaras,</u> or 'fordfinders', of whom Mohavira was the last."(30) By the way, Jainism has always insisted that each person must do the "fordfinding" alone without the help of any God. Thus Jainism honours Mahavira and the long line of twenty-three <u>tirthankaras</u> before him; particularly notable is the historical figure of Parshva, who is honoured as the twenty-third "fordfinder" ca.872--772 B.C. (cf. Zimmer, op. cit, p. 183)

Jainism is known as an extreme system even within its Indian environment for its monotheism, its asceticism and its extreme devotion to ahimsa (the ethic of non-injury). Western students of the world's religions are often puzzled by the attitudes of indifference and denial of God which are to be found among the Eastern religions. Hutchison says, "Jainism goes beyond indifference and agnosticism to an unqualified denial that any deity created or rules the world. True, it concedes the existence of superior power, but it asserts that these superior powers, like human beings, are prisoners within this evil universe with little or no chance of escape."(31) Since the Western term atheism is considered by some as misleading, a new term called Transpolytheistic atheism has been suggested, meaning precisely a rejection of any deity as creator and ruler of the world. Along with Jainism, Goshala of the Ajivikas asserted a similar denial. Now the question is: What led them to reject the existence of God(s)? There are two possibilities: First, they thought the existence of gods is unnecessary, for men could achieve salvation through their own work and power without "neurotic" dependence on gods outside their jurisdiction. Secondly, the gods appeared even at that early time of human history to be an irrational principle of explanation.

Asceticism (tapas) is one of the common practices and most popular in the Indian religions. But the Jains practise it in an extreme way. For example, some of the greatest Jaina saints are known to have ended their lives by fasting to death. The Jaina monks traditionally have worn a piece of "cheesecloth" over the mouth to prevent swallowing bugs, thereby destroying live insects, and have carried a small broom to sweep living things from their path.

Obviously, in these practices there is an approach to asceticism and non-injury to living beings. The latter may be considered to be based upon the idea of the unity of all life and the feeling of reverence for life. Admittedly, the Jaina doctrine of ahimsa has certainly affected Hindu tradition and was accepted and practised by Mahatma Gandhi as an influence on his personal, ethical thinking. "Yet Jainism's own extremes of practice are vividly summarized in a paragraph by Heinrich Zimmer"(32).

Today, the Jaina community is still alive with its practices and tradition. The community consists of approximately 1,680,000 people.(33) The Jaina Community has contributed to Indian culture. As a result, Indian ethics, philosophy, literature, architecture and even sculpture all show considerable Jaina influence. The life and the religio-cultural contribution of the twenty-four Jaina founders of whom Mahavira stands out as the most influential, is the net-result of the still-alive Jainism.(34)

Heinrich Zimmer thinks that Jainism developed in a tradition of ideas and attitudes going back to Indian's ancient past. Apart of Zimmer's evidence is the realist and pluralist outlook of Jaina philosophy, in contrast of the monistic idealism. Thus realism and pluralism, Zimmer claims, stand for the philosophic outlook of the pre-Aryan (Dravidian) people.

The system of thinking which has formed the fundamental of Jainism could be called as a philosophy of salvation. It is a group of general ideas about human life and the world which will guide a person's way along the hard and difficult path out of the world's misery to salvation. This is what Jainism claims without being able to find what Mahavira exactly said; still Jainas maintain that the Jaina record shows that Mahavira was the original philosopher who said it.

(L) <u>The Way of Salvation</u>

The Jaina view is that people are to be freed from attachment to this world of misery, to the blessedness called <u>Kevala/Kaivalya</u> (separation); that means, a release from mortal enslavement of this world. It is completed in a "supernatural" sphere of bliss called "<u>isatpragbhara</u>, at the top of the universe".

That is to say, "continued individual existence rather than absorption".(Schoeps, op. cit.. p. 89).

Interestingly, Jainism has a five-fold classification of living beings according to their number of senses. Thus humans, gods and demons, which have five senses, are classified together. A second class contains creatures of four senses—touch, taste, smell and sight. The three-sense creature includes such small organisms as fleas, ants and moths. Two-sense creatures includes warms, leaches and shellfish. The one-sense beings are a huge class including vegetable bodies ranging from trees to turnips, earth bodies which include stones, clay and jewels, water bodies, fire bodies and wind bodies. That means, according to the Jaina philosophy, the whole world is alive. One author considers this view as "hylozoism."(35) In a nutshell, "Every object contains a soul which is imprisoned in wretchedness within its body, grooming in misery, vainly seeking escape. This cosmic misery is regarded as the inexorable working of the iron law of Karma."(36)

It should be mentioned here that Jainism, like other oriental philosophies, for instance, Buddhism, maintains that this world has no beginning and no end. The world exists for ever as a kind of permanent universal vessel for the misery of its creatures. For human beings alone there is a chance of salvation. The situation or condition of humanity is a kind of escape or get free opening from the world. Thus, one Jaina religious poem bids its readers: "After tossing on the ocean of being, of which birth and death are waves, you have come to man's estate. Avoid the things of sense and pluck the fruit of human birth."(37)

In passing, it may be mentioned here that Jainism is undoubtedly an ascetic way of life, and the manner in which emancipation may be achieved is by the practice of <u>tapas</u> and <u>ahimsa</u>.(38).

Finally, Jainism has laid down twelve vows for ordinary adherents, especially less strict than those of the monks: (1) never knowingly to take the life of a sentient being, (2) never to lie, (3) never to steal, (4) never to be unchaste, (5) to check greed, (6) to avoid temptations, (7) to limit the number of things in daily use, (8) to guard against all available evil, (9) to keep stated periods of meditation, 10) to observe periods of self-denial, (11) to spend occasional periods as a monk, and (12) to give alms.(39)

(M) <u>Sikhism</u>

The founder of this socio-religious and political community was Nanak (1469-1539), born and brought up in Talwandi, near Lahore, Punjab (now in Pakistan). For a long time this area of the then India had been a place for Hindu

24

and Muslim meeting and mingling, but unfortunately, also for fighting between these two communities. It is for this reason that Nanak raised his voice in protest against religious conflict.

There was an important religious platform, an organisation called the Bhakti Movement headed by a famed devotee named Kabir—the Bhakta (1440-1518). The Bhakti devotees went around the countryside singing their songs of faith. Sufis (Muslim mystics) also went around singing God's names and praise to Him. To an ordinary person like Nanak, those devotional traditions must have seemed indistinguishable. Sometimes their followers worshipped at the same place and marched in the same processions.

Interestingly, many of these saints raised their voices on common issues. For example, they protested against religious conflict and empty ceremonialism and stood for human brotherhood. Hindu Bhaktas protested against the caste system. Famous among these Bhaktas were the fifteenth-century Ramananda and his well-known disciple, Kabir—the Bhakta, mentioned above, who described himself as "a child of Rama and Allah", and devoted himself to the reconciliation of Hindu and Muslim.(40). Kabir found no difficulty in believing in one God, the Supreme reality, beside whom all else was illusion. He also believed that each person must find his/her way to God with the guidance of a <u>guru</u> as well as by meditation and singing hymns of praise and love. Kabir had a group of disciples, and Nanak was one of them. Over five hundred of Kabir's hymns have been incorporated into the <u>Adi Granth.</u> Kabir's tradition of devotion influenced the development of Sikhism in many ways, not least of all in the Sikh emphasis on a personal teacher (<u>guru</u>).

Nanak's parents were Hindus. His school master was a Muslim. Nanak was a meditative child who married at the age of twelve but failed to turn his mind toward more family life. He had two sons. His father tried to settle him into a stable occupation, but he failed as a cowherd and as a businessman. Leaving his family, he went to the district capital Sultanpur where he became the manger of government store. He was met there by a Muslim friend and musician, Mardana, and the two jointly organised a group for the singing of hymns, which eventually became a group of religious searchers.

A great crisis in Nanak's life happened one day as he was bathing in the river before going to his work. According to the Sikh account, God gave him a cup of "nectar" to drink and spoke to him in the following words: "Nanak, I am with thee. Through thee will my name be magnified; whosoever follows thee, him will I save. Go into the world to pray and teach mankind how to pray. Be not sullied by the ways of the God. Let your life be one of praise of the word, charity, ablution, service and prayer. Nanak, I give thee my pledge. Let this be thy life's mission.(41).

In reply to the divine call, Nanak spoke the words which introduce the "Japji, the_morning prayer" which is repeated quietly each morning by every religious Sikh to this day:

There is one God.

He is the supreme truth.

He, the creator,

Is without fear and without hate.

He, the omnipresent,

Pervades the universe.

He in not born,

Nor does He die to be born again.

By His grace shalt thou worship Him.

Before time itself

There was truth.

When time began to run its course

He was the truth.

Even now, He is the truth.

Ever more shalt truth prevail (42).

The divine voice uttered again, telling to Nanak: "Thou art the Guru, the Supreme Guru of God". At this time Nanak is reported to have received the "robe of honour [long outer garment] from the God who spoke to him." In the meantime, he was reported missing, and it was thought that he was "drowned" in the river. On the fourth day, he came back home and gave away all his personal belongings save a loincloth. From the multitude, he disappeared quietly. Then he went with Mardana, his friend, and joined a few of beggars. On the following day, he stood up and spoke, telling only: "There is no Hindu and no Mussalman." (43).

This all-important experience took place in 1499, during Nanak's thirteenth year." Following these experiences, Nanak was ready to leave, accompanied by Mardana, to announce the truth he had received.

(N) <u>Nanak's Teachings</u>

The record of Sikh teaching is the <u>Adi Granth</u>, a well-known collection and compilation of the teaching of Nanak, of the gurus, of Kabir and of many other Sikh, Hindu and Muslim religious teachers. It should be mentioned here that the tenth guru, Gobind Singh, declared that after him there would be no more gurus, but the Granth would serve this function for the Sikh community. That is exactly what has been going on.

Nanak's fundamental teaching was: "God the True Name". The designation <u>True Name</u> was in part his intention to rise above such limiting and factional names as Shiva, Rama and Allah, even though some times he did not hesitate to use these names. Further, there are "devotional" practice in both Islam and Hinduism which focused on the devotee's attention on the names of God. Nanak's poems also contain monotheistic features such as <u>sovereign</u>, <u>creator</u> and <u>lord</u>. There are also several terms, such as <u>love</u>, sometimes loudly extreme love, which were common to both Sufi and Bhakti traditions or practices.

As for the God's relation to the world, Nanak spoke by turns of both Maya and creation. For example, he spoke the following :

> Maya, the mythical goddess,
> Sprang from the One,
> And her womb brought forth
> Three acceptable disciples of the One:
> Brahma, Vishnu and Shiva.(44).

Commenting on the above saying of Nanak, Hutchison says: "Nanak's view of Maya seems to have been that of the deceptive force of illusion pervading all things other than the One. Yet alongside such references, and indeed much more frequent, the reader finds references to the world as the work and creation of the sovereign monotheistic Lord of all."(45)

One important teaching of Nanak, drawn from both Hindu and Muslim sources, is that there is a need for a guru who works hard to maintain a personal relation with his students. Nanak emphasised the need for a guru. The guidance of a guru is both required and enough to lead men to God:

> O Man, repeat God's name and praises;
> But how shalt thou obtain this pleasure without
> the Guru?
> It is the guru who uniteth man with God.(46).

Again there are references to foreordained destiny, yet some writers emphasise that "Nanak's view was that human freedom under God conquers fate and predestination."(47). In short, here is the teaching of "monotheistic freedom". Yet Nanak also clearly taught the Hindu doctrine of Karma-Samsara, emphasizing that sinful conduct led to the slavery of perpetual rebirths, while compliance led liberation or mukti.

The word Sikh means "disciple." The Sikh gurus have also been distinctive leaders of their people in war and peace and politics. Sikhism has communicated its peculiar definition to the word <u>guru</u>. Nanak abandoned many of the Hindu forms by which God is "mediated to humans".

In this dogma of humanity, Nanak managed to put together a view of human excellence and satisfaction with a strong perception or feeling of sin, foolishness and evil. Thus Nanak said: "Numberless are the ways of folly and vice."(48).

By the way, Nanak's ethical and social teachings explained many of his lifelong beliefs: First and most remarkable, he never tired of criticizing worthless ceremonialism in religion, as well as religious divisions or classes such as caste which he believed to inconsistent with human morality or honesty. There is a story about Nanak that "when on the banks of the Ganges, he saw Hindus throwing water to the rising sun as an offering to their ancestors, he turned and began to throw water in the opposite direction. When asked what he was doing, he replied that he was watering his fields at home in the Punjab. For, he said, if these people could send water to heaven surely he could send it surely to his home village."(49) Nanak never failed to say that religion consists not only of things like this, but of deeds of kindness and goodness. Sometimes Nanak used to say the traditional Indian word <u>ahimsa</u> for this moral quality.

One important feature of Nanak's teaching is his rejection of asceticism. He lived a worldly life and asked his followers to do the same way. However, while Nanak asked his followers to live within the world, he prescribed a strict and orderly self-control way of personal uprightness for them. As long as in the world, it was nonetheless at first a clearly quiet way of life. However, this tradition which Nanak left behind to his followers was destined within a period of two centuries to be changed into a severe, fighting faith (especially against the Muslim rulers of the Indian sub-continent for Sikh leaders dreamt of an independent Punjab state).

It should be mentioned here that Guru Ram Das is noted in history for beginning both the famous Golden Temple at Amritsar and the city around the temple. He also sent missionaries to many parts of India. His son, Guru Arjun, proved to be one of the greatest and most active of all the gurus. He completed the temple and also the tank of Amritsar, making bathing a sacred ritual. He completed the <u>Adi Granth</u> and installed it in the temple. Also, it was he whose political aspiration was the main cause of Mughal Emperor Jahangir's anger not only against him which ended in his death, but also against the Sikh community, particularly for its political aspiration within the boundary of the Muslim-Indian Empire(50).

The last guru, Gobind Singh took a constructive step "for himself and for the Sikhs when in 1699 he instituted the <u>Khalsa</u> or the Community of the Pure, by a new ritual called the <u>baptism of the sword</u> . The sacred rite began after the morning worship when the guru appeared before the assembled multitude, took out his sword, and demanded five men for sacrifice. After some delay, one volunteer offered himself. He was taken into a tent, and a little later the guru reappeared with his sword dropping blood from it and asked for another volunteer, and so on to the number of five. After that the guru produced the five goats he had sacrificed and gathered the five men for a new ritual of initiation, or "baptismal ceremony."(51). Then he asked the five men to drink from a single container. Since they had come from different Hindu castes, this meant their initiation into the casteless community of the <u>khalsa</u>. Their Hindu names were changed to the name of Singh (lion), and they recited the "martial creed of the <u>khalsa</u>". Five symbols of "k" were readied: (1) <u>kesh</u> (unshaven hair and bread), (2) <u>kangha</u> (comb to keep the hair tidy), (3) <u>Kacha</u> (knee-length breeches), (4) <u>Kara</u> (a steel bracelet on the right wrist), and (5) <u>Kirpan</u> (the saber). "Four rules were prescribed: (1) not to cut any hair of the body, (2) not to smoke or chew tobacco or drink alcohol, (3) not to eat meat of any animal slaughtered by the customary Muslim bleeding to death, (4) not to molest Muslim women or to have sexual relations with any women except a lawful wife. Having admitted the five khalsa, Gobind asked them in turn to baptize him, to demonstrate their equality with him in the new brotherhood."(52)

Thus began the new trained order of fighting Sikh. Guru Gobind made membership in this new "brotherhood" open to all who wanted to join; thus came around him a group of brave warriors. In the following years, there were many occasions to test their strength and skill of actual fighting, for Gobind and his fighter-followers spent their lives in continued but unsuccessful conflict with the Mughal rulers of India. The change from peaceful sect to a fighting "theocracy" remained in effect unsuccessful, for the Muslim rule in India came to an end in 1858 as a result of severe battle between the Muslims and the British East Indian forces, not certainly between the Muslims and the Sikhs, even though the latter supported the British.

As for Guru Gobind's life, it was spent in life-threatening and sorrowful combat. In 1704, after three years of siege, his headquarters at Anandpur fell to the armies of Mughal Emperor Aurangzeb. His mother and his two youngest sons were among the victims. Gobind escaped to fight again at Chamkaur, where again his forces including his two remaining sons perished.

Gobind himself escaped and fled to the Deccan, where later re-joined with Bahadur Shah, who expressed interest in him and his cause. He spent the remaining days of his life with Bahadur Shah but was murdered at Nanded by a Muslim. The place of Gobind's death, Nanded, has become a Sikh pilgrimage spot.

Following Guru Gobind's time, Sikh history was full of chaos and religio-political turmoil until a great leader, Ranjit Singh, appeared on the scene. He succeeded in carving out a Sikh Kingdom which included almost the whole of the Punjab. But his kingdom did not last beyond his death in 1839. Ranjit's most formidable enemy was the British who wanted to establish their power all over India, rather than the Muslims. British diplomacy and arms checked Ranjit's expansion, and after his death British arms brought the Sikhs within British India.(53)

(O) <u>Buddha and Early Buddhism (Indian)</u>

It may be stated at the outset that Buddha belongs along with Mahavira (discussed before) to the "axis age" of Indian history. Naturally, there are important similarities in the biographies and teachings of these two "mystic-philosophers". They were born and lived in the same north-eastern region of India. There are other similarities between them: Both were nobles born to rule; both renounced the throne for the austere or strict life of the religious ascetic, seeking and finally finding release. "Both were rebels against hardening caste lines and increasing Brahman domination of Indian religion and life, with the result that later ages of Hinduism judged both men heretics. Indeed, so similar are their biographies that some observers have concluded Buddha and Mahavira were the same man."(54)

Notwithstanding the above-mentioned facts, there are significant differences as well, as we will see later. While both were bravely original philosophic-mystical minded, their teachings differ fundamentally. While both started austere monastic movements, Jainism is a way of "extreme asceticism"; Buddhism, in contrast, has described itself as a "middle way" to salvation. For this and other reasons, these two religions have developed in different ways.

It is interesting to describe briefly Buddha's life: Buddha was born to a noble family in the region of Magadha of north-east India, (the present state of Bihar) in approximately 560-480 B. C. His life stories, mostly legendary, have been recorded in the Jataka tales of which approximately 550 exist. Buddhist tradition also records stories of Buddha's miraculous birth. In a dream, his mother is said to have seen a heavenly white elephant with a lotus flower in its trunk, who appeared and entered her side.(55)

Brahman astrologers prophesised that the child would see what Buddhism has called the four passing sights which would wake him to the joyless facts of human misery. Accordingly, his father took every possible preventive measure to protect him from the world. He was brought up in luxury and was set apart to succeed his father on the throne. He was married to his cousin, Yashodhara. They had a son named Rahula (fetter). Yet, he still wanted separation.

Prince Siddhartha was not internally happy with his princely life. At the age of twenty-nine, his dissatisfaction with the worldly life came to light. Despite precautions, one day he saw the four passing sights,---an old man, a sick man, a dead man and a monk. The first three told to the future Buddha the sadness of human life, and the fourth symbolised release from it. Siddhartha's mind was made up. Heedless of his father's efforts to change his mind by means of parties with dancing and singing girls, he got up a servant and rode off into the night. Having gone far, he came down, took off his clothes, cut off his hair, and put on the minimum clothes of a "wandering ascetic". That was what Buddhist tradition called the <u>great renunciation</u> or the <u>great retirement.</u>. Thus began Buddha's seven-year of seeking for salvation.(56)

He began with extreme asceticism. We are told that one day, worn out from hunger, he fainted. His fellow ascetics thought he was dead. After regaining consciousness, he realized that that way too was futile. After taking a little food, he gained strength. The other ascetics deserted him disappointed. "Yet Siddhartha was actually on the threshold of the great discovery which would make him the 'enlightened one', or the Buddha".(57)

According to some traditional accounts, the Buddha-to-be also made his way through the "six superknowledge and the three cognitions". A traditional list of the former is: (1) magic powers, (2) the divine ear, (3) knowing other minds, (4) memory of past incarnations, (5) the divine-eye, and (6) extinction of sensual desire and of ignorance. The three cognitions are (1) of one's previous existences (2) of the whole world of death and rebirth, and (3) of the happy consequences of good deeds and the miserable consequences of evil deeds in the round of life. Achievement of the sixth super-knowledge and the third cognition yielded the four noble truths: (1) the truth of suffering, (2) the source of suffering, (3) the cessation of suffering and (4) the noble eight-fold path of this goal. "The meditating Siddhartha was now the Buddha—in traditional etymology, the 'enlightened one', but in more accurate etymology, the 'awakened one'. He had achieved his goal."(58)

It is stated that involvement in the aforesaid climatic or prevailing experience was also the discovery of the law called 'pratityasamutpada' "the law of dependent arising", "dependent origination" or simply, "the twelve preconditions" that is, of mortal existence."(59) However, when translated this principle, discovered by the Buddha himself, asserts a twelve-fold chain of causation at the end of which is the world of mortal misery. Conversely, by breaking its first link—ignorance (avidya)—the Buddha broke successively the whole chain. The twelve links of the chain of preconditions are (1) ignorance, (2) dispositions, (3) consciousness, (4)name and from, (5) the six sense fields, (6) contact, (7) feeling, (8) craving, (9) appropriation, (10) becoming, (11) birth, and (12) aging and dying.

The figurative expression of chain as well as the necessities of revelation make this principle sound easier. Some statements of Buddha's meditation and awakening emphasize that "he began with the twelfth link of the chain and working backward to the first". At any rate, "his climatic experience and thought under the bo tree broke the chain and solved the problem of mortal misery"(60).

Certainly, Buddha's noble eight-fold path is understood as the "middle way to nirvana", being the way between the two extremes of Jaina asceticism, on the one hand, and luxury, on the other. This eight-fold path is the following: (1) right understanding, (2) right mindedness, (3) right speech, (4) right action, (5) right livelihood, (6) right effort, (7) right meditation and (8) right emancipation.

The first two steps have to do with understanding and the disposition of the human mind toward the Buddhist way; they are called the <u>higher wisdom</u>. The next three taken together form the <u>ethical disciplines</u>; the last three steps are called the <u>mental disciplines</u> for, based upon the preceding ones, "they prepare, direct, and then move the seeking mind onward to the achievement of its goal, nirvana" (61).

The importance of "this experience of awakening in the life of Buddha" and of everyone who used it in his life is for good and all to break the "iron-chain of <u>Karma-samsara</u>" (the cycle of rebirths). Buddhists believe that Buddha's great understanding opened a new chapter in the history of human spiritual life. Once this path to <u>nirvana</u> (salvation) had been found and opened up by Buddha, other persons might also follow it. By the way, Buddha himself openly denied that <u>nirvana</u> meant "annihilation", what is annihilated is only the unconscious desire which causes suffering. Then what is left is bliss beyond the understanding of all save those who know it by direct experience.

Buddhist tradition narrates Buddha's subsequent meditation for another seven weeks during which he went through a period of doubt as to whether this fresh knowledge should be announced to the public. The question was whether, having experienced <u>nirvana</u>, he should immediately seek its full realisation (a situation which Buddhists call <u>parinirvana</u> and believed that for sure, he achieved at death) or whether out of sympathy for suffering people, he should tell others the happy news of relief from suffering. The later option was adopted, and the Buddha commenced what is turned out to be "a forty-five year mission."(62).

He delivered a sermon first to five former fellow ascetics in the Deer Park near Banares, thus beginning the wheel of the <u>dharma</u>. As it is well known, the Buddha's preaching was an explanation of the "four noble truths and the noble eight-fold path". These men formed the base of the <u>Sangha</u> (Buddhist monastic order). Buddha sent them all out in all directions to preach and teach the new way of <u>nirvana</u> (relief or deliverance).

Each new monk took the vow which has become traditional throughout the Buddhist domain. "I take refuge in the Buddha, the Dharma and the Sangha". Members of the order were bound together by a common discipline and by their saffron robes, and of course, by their common allegiance to Buddha. The discipline is summerised in the traditional ten maxims: (1) I take the vow not to destroy life, (2) I take the vow not to steal, (3) I take the vow to abstain from impurity, (4) I take the vow not to lie, (5) I take the vow to abstain from intoxicating drinks, (6) I take the vow not to eat at forbidden times; (7) I take the vow to abstain from dancing, singing, music and stage plays, (8) I take the vow not to use garlands, scents, unguents or ornaments, (9) I take the vow not to use high or broad bed, (10) I take the now not to receive gold or silver.(63).

It may be pointed out here that his own complete adoption of this new system was not all, for on returning home, Buddha converted his royal father, his wife and son, and other members of the court, including his cousin, Devadhatta.

It should be mentioned that the <u>Sangha</u> was a democracy, "the earliest monastic institution governed by perfect democratic principles which continued all the way to present day(64).

The Buddha's death (<u>Parinirvana</u>) occurred at the age of eighty at Kusinara. His last words are reported to be: "And now, O priest, I take my leave of you; all the constituents of being are transitory; work out your salvation with diligence."(65)

(P) <u>Buddha's Teachings</u>

We have already discussed some of the important teachings in summarising his life, for it is a notable fact that his life and his teaching are inseparably bound together. As we have examined, the basis of his message to humans was his discernment into the nature of mortal suffering and its cure. Suffering or misery (<u>dukkha</u>) is rooted in ignorance and hankering to be and to get. Ignorance (<u>avidya</u>) about the true state of reality leads to craving or longing, which in turn attributes reality to transitory and unreal things. If this root of senseless or ignorant longing is cut, the whole huge tree of misery will fade and die. What is left is not dead—though it will appear so to those ignorant minds still held fast in their attachment to the world. Rather it is the perfect happiness of <u>Nirvana</u>, not actually negative, but "superaffirmative." ("Coomaraswamy has coined the term "despirated' for Nirvana, as the negative of "aspirated "). Such, at least, is the understanding of Buddha's followers(66).

(Q) <u>Tibbetan Buddhism</u>

After some time, to advance its missionary zeal, Buddhism found its way to Tibet during the reign of King Songstan-Gampo, whose reign begun in 632 A.D. He bound together both Indian and Chinese civilizations when he married two Buddhist girls belonging to these two civilizations. He collected Buddhist books from these two civilizations.

The native religion, "called <u>Bonism</u> (or <u>ponism</u>), was a kind of polydemonism" devoted to appeasing the spirits of that hopeless and harsh land. "It featured animal sacrifice and some- times human sacrifice, and other ritual offerings to the spirits. Magic words and magic dances were all part of a pattern of averting the damage that evil or capricious spirits could bring to people"(67). After some years of debate between the pro-Buddhists and those who wanted the old way, the appearance of the two Indian <u>gurus</u>, namely, Shantarakshita and Padmasambhava, the latter is an expert in <u>Tantrism</u>, initiated the founding of the Tibetan Buddhist <u>Sangha</u> and its first monastery. "Shantarakshita was a characteristic celibate scholar monk, while Padmasambhava was a wonder-working guru practicing neither celibacy nor attached to monastic regimen. Tibetan Buddhism, it is well-known, has always been interacting between these two models (68).

During the ninth and tenth centuries, the translation of Buddhist scriptures from Sanskrit into Tibetan as well as the involvement of Buddhism in the mean politics of the country took place. There were also continuous movements of anti-Buddhist persecution.

The Indian scholar and tantric master Atisha (982-1054) went to Tibet in 1042, to give tantric "instruction and initiation" and also establishing a "monastery and an order of monks". After him, Marpa (1012-1077) and Milarepa (1040-1123) became the first and second patriarchs of the Kargyupa sect. Milarepa was both a saint and a poet of Tibet; his poetry has been translated into English.(69)

The type of Buddhism which took form in Tibet has been in many ways unique and different from those of other countries. The title lama (one who is superior) was given both to chief monks as well as important house owner yogins. The monks dwell in thick-walled monasteries made for protection against Tibet's severe weather conditions. However, within these walls, tantric beliefs and practices often replaced monastic celibacy and more "traditional" or usual forms of contemplation. Like all other monastic movements, worldliness and reform have alternated in Tibbetan Buddhism (Atisha, Marpa and Milarepa were well-known reformers).

At the popular level, Tibbetan Buddhism has concerned itself with holy devices, such as Om mani padme hum, and with religious devices, for example, thangkas (mandalas) and the prayer wheel, while containing a prayer which is addressed to the buddhas each in turn. Some Tibetans have had their prayer wheels turned by water power, and there are reports of prayer wheels even run by electricity.

At a higher position, Buddhism exchanged idea with Tibetan culture to produce special forms of thought and devotion. The main text, is the Bardo Thotrol ("Tibetan Book of the Dead"). Tibetan tradition considers it to belong to Padma Sambhava, and he is said to have buried it so that the future generations might recover it and live accordingly.

To modern readers, the book containing a characteristic way of life assume the main group of ideas we have seen in Mahayana and Vajrayana Buddhism. There is the highest goal of liberation (enlightenment); there is the ever present fact of Karma-Samsara (transmigration); there are the hosts of buddhas and badhisattvas with the tantric grouping of male and female deities, and there is the guidance of sacred words, mandalas and ceremonies.

Finally, it should be mentioned, there is an event which Tibetan Buddhists remember with self-esteem: the appointment by the Chinese Emperor, Kublai Khan of the Grand abbot of Tibetan Buddhism as Kuo-shih (instructor of the nation). This abbot, Phakpa by name, was also given by Kublai Khan supreme authority over all Tibet, making him the first lama to be sovereign ruler of the country.(70).

(R) <u>Zoroastrianism (Parseeism)</u>

The Parsees (Iranians) of India, the Bodins (Gabars) of Iran are the only surviving followers of Zoroastrianism, the smallest of the world's living religions. This community located mainly in and around Mumbai, India. Presently, they are a very wealthy commercial community.

Though small, it is the recipient of a great tradition. Its founder, Zoroaster (Zarathustra), was one of the great figures of the "axis" of the seventh and sixth centuries B.C. From that time until the coming of Islam in the early seventh century (642 C.E.), Zoroastrianism was the religion of the vast Sassanid (Persian) Empire. From Persia it reached out in many directions and influenced other peoples and their religions. "Both Judaism and Christianity show Zoroastrian influences in the figure of Satan and in the hosts of angels surrounding both God and Satan. Zoroastrian gods, symbols, and cults made their way into the ancient Greco-Roman world—Mithras being only the best known of many deities of Iranian origin. The cult of Manichaeism, which was one of the evils of early Christianity, and one of influences on the thought of Saint Augustine, was apparently a heretical Zoroastrian sect."(71).The religious environment of ancient Persia was remarkably similar to that of Vedic India. However, the appearance of the "prophet" Zoroaster with a religion represents a direction independent of other religions of that time.

Like Judaism, Christianity and Islam, Zoroastrianism is a religion of a book—a fact of extreme significance historically and theologically. For example, even a superficial reading of the Zoroastrian "Bible", called the Avesta, makes it clear that the reader is in a different religious environment from southern or eastern Asia. This book speaks of the One God whose sovereign will is that all people should serve him, and serve no other gods. In other words, with the exception of Sikhism, Zoroastrianism is the first example of monotheism (a part from the Semitic religion, of course).

In addition to the frequent mention of the figurative image of sovereignty for deity, we read in the Avesta the repeated occurring image of hearing. God speaks, and humans hear and act. "The predominance of the metaphor of hearing over that of seeing may be said to define a religion of revelation. Revelation implies that humans do not have within their own minds and selves the meaning of life, and that therefore God must disclose it to them. Hence God speaks, disclosing himself and his will to humankind; the role of humans is to hear and do the will of God."(72). From this, the next step is to put down in black and white what is heard, and this, of course, becomes the guide for all life.

Zoroaster presents himself as a "prophet" who had the deep conviction that God called him and asked him to deliver

His message to humans. His faith emerged in the midst of an ancient Iranian religion which appears to be very similar to Vedic Indian religion. "If this is true", says Hutchison, "the diverging religious developments in India and Iran constitute one of the most remarkable contrasts in humankinds' religious history. The mountains which separate India and Iran have been the great divide separating religions of the second and third types."(73).

Later Zoroastrianism is reported to have developed the principle of moral and cosmic dualism. For us the question is this: In what terms do we understand this dualism and its relation to Zoroastrian monotheism? What, in other words, are the relations between the good Ahura Mazda and the evil Angra Mainyu?

A different kind of issue is raised by the historical sources of Zoroastrianism. Scholarly attempts at a reconstruction of the main issues are limited. Therefore, an abstract list of the main parts of the Avesta and other Zoroastrian sources is needed for the exposition.

The oldest and most reliable parts of the Avesta are the Gathas (hymns of Zoroaster). These hymns are attributed to Zoroaster himself and together them constitute the innermost part of the yasna, the Avesta contains four other principal subdivisions: a shorter liturgy called the Visp-rat (Vispered); the

Yashts (invocation); the <u>Khurda Avesta</u> ("little Avesta": a series of hymns addressed to many deities); and, finally, the <u>Videvdat/ Venididad</u> or"law against demons", which is concerned mainly with problems of ritual purity(74).

In addition to the Avesta, there are other texts and archeologicalmaterials,includinganimportantseriesofinscriptions from the well-known Achaemenid kings for instance Darius and Xerxes, which also give information about Zoroastrianism during their times. From a later date, approximately the third through ninth centuries, appears a series of texts in the Pahlavi language, composed mainly of translations and commentaries on earlier records. "These primary sources are supplemented by comments of historians", especially of Herodotus. There is the widest disagreement concerning the date of Zoroaster's life(75).

It should be mentioned here that Zoroastrian tradition has glorified the life history of its founder. He is said to have received the sacred thread at fifteen. He was a youth dutiful to his parents and of a compassionate nature. Yet at the age of twenty, he left his home and hearth to wonder into the world alone in search of answers to his religious questions. One source asserts that he kept a seven-year silence, living in a cave during this entire time(76).

(S) Zoroastra's Message (Divine Revelation)

The core of Zoroaster's message was faith in One God, Ahura Mazda, who had revealed his will to him and through the prophet to mankind. Zoroaster took stand firmly on the revelation which he received, as he claimed, confident that God Himself had disclosed to him the faith which he believed. This firm belief and predisposition defined his role as a prophet or spokesman for God. "This fresh revelation", says a writer, "was doubtless related to the newly developing world to which Zoroastrian addressed himself. Furthermore, if this faith was of divine origin, alternative, diverging faiths had to be accounted false and evil. Zoroaster did not shrink from denouncing them as such"(77). From this statement, we see in Zoroastrianism a characteristic feature of monotheistic religion. This feature was absent in the earlier religions.

(T) The One God

The One God whom he proclaimed was called Ahura Mazda (Wise Lord/Lord of Right). Ahura Mazda bears significant similarity to the Indian Vedic god Varuna. The Gathas leave no doubt that Zoroaster regarded Ahura Mazda as the "One Sovereign Lord of Creation". His will determines the model of all creation. "Lordship also meant creatorship; the Gathas tell the story of divine creation in which Ahura Mazda called the world

51

into being in the beginning. Like his biblical contemporary, Deutero-Isaiah, Zoroaster asked rhetorically:

> Who set the Earth in its place below
> and the sky of the clouds that it shall not fall?
> Who the waters and planets?
> Who yoked the two steeds to wind and clouds?
> Who O wise One is the creator of the Good
>   Mind?
> What artificer made light and darkness?
> What artificer sleep and waking?
> Who made morning, moon and night?
> To remind the wise man of his task?
> Thus I strive to recognise in thee, O Wise One
> As Holy Spirit, the Creator of all things(78).

(U)<u>Angels</u>

Zoroaster's monotheism was qualified by many forms which are variously interpreted as angels or messengers, heavenly attendants or servants, divine attributes, or at times simply personifications(79).

(V) Duality of Good and Evil

Deriving from the lordship of Ahura Mazda together with the dualism, noted above, is Zoroaster's unique view of all history as a continuous war between good and evil. There are good and evil persons just as there are good and evil spirits. It is believed that the evil spirits (daevas) have joined together with "Angra Mainyu" to oppose Ahura Mazda and his large number of good spirits. In this war, humans are urged to join the forces of Ahura Mazda against the evil spirits; humans will be able to do good works like "tilling the soil, raising grains irrigating" lands being kind to animals. The "arch-villains" of this game of "good and evil are the Turanian nomads who worship the evil daevas, slaughter animals and destroy the grain of the field. "The end of this war is Judgment Day when the sovereignty of Ahura Mazda will be fully vindicated. Zoroaster seems to have believed that the struggle of good and evil was an actual and often a desperate fight. Yet, paradoxically, at no point did he doubt the final victory of Ahura Mazda." (80).

(W) Later Zoroastrianism

Turning from the Gathas of Zoroaster to later Avesta (the Yashts, the Khurda Avesta), and the Pahlavi texts, we get into a different situation. Significant changes have been made in the Zoroastrian religion because generations after Zoroaster, the famous Cyrus came to power two centuries later beginning the Achaemenid dynasty which lasted until Alexander came. In 558 B.C. Cyrus brought the Median and Persian kingdoms together into the Medo-Persian Empire. He was a Zoroastrian, but as an empire-builder he was willing to bring about understanding among religions for the sake of peace amongst the many groups of people disposed widespread territories.

One of the Cyrus' successors was Darius (522-486 B.C.E.) whose inspirations show him to have been a devout Zoroastrian ruling by the will of Ahura Mazda and seeking the same justice and virtuous regime declared by Zoroaster. But in the case of Xerxes (486-568 B.C.E.), there were several important changes. One inscription records his suppression of the Daeva cult, a work of the original Zoroastrianism, but others speak about large scale animal sacrifice. "Xerxes is also said to have lashed the waters of the Hellespont during his attempted invasion of Greece, calling them bitter waters."(81).This was a work some authors describe as inconsistent with Zoroastrian veneration for water. Additional deities like god Mithra and goddess Anahita reappeared.

(X) Deification of Zoroaster

Most important feature of Zoroastrianism is the deification of Zoroaster himself. "In the <u>Gathas</u>, Zoroaster appears as a man, listening to Ahura Mazda, talking back sometimes, but always declaring Ahura Mazda's will to humankind. In the latter writings he is depicted as a supernatural being, a veritable god become man. His coming has been foretold 3,000 years previously. The demons are forewarned and quake in their impending overthrow."(82). It may also be mentioned that not only Zoroaster's birth but also that of his mother is miraculous. It is also reported that as he was born, he was attacked by the demons—and is miraculously saved by different forces of goodness. Zoroaster himself carried out many wonders. "The great miracle of the cure of Vishtaspa's horse is elaborated in detail. Every aspect of the prophet's life is fitted into a framework of popular supernaturalism—a process of which the history of religions affords numerous illustrations."(83).

Before moving to another subject, let us say a few words concerning Zoroaster's efforts towards the religious reform which seems to be peculiar compared with other religious reforms we are familiar with. We are told that Zoroaster's religious reform, and his hard work against sacrifices, was related to his high respect for animals, and particularly his whole-hearted "love" for the cow, which in those days was the main animal for sacrifice. For this reason, some academics have treated Zoroaster's reform efforts as showing the influence of the peasants upon the shaping the Persian (Iranian) religion. We are also told that Zoroaster "proclaimed the sanctity of the cow; in his religion the eating of the flesh of cattle is forbidden even more strictly than the eating of pork among the Jews and the Muslims. Moreover, the imagery in which Zoroaster describes the kingdom of God is drawn from peasant life. 'To win the cow," is a synonym for heavenly bliss; "to drink sweet milk," for supreme joy; "to enter the promised land of rich pasture," "for entry into paradise"(84).

(Y) Angels and Deities

Although Zoroaster's monotheism accepted a few angels and other heavenly beings, there were certain limits. But in later Zoroastrianism those limits were crossed by a variety of gods and Goddesses and heavenly messengers. Many of the former Persian "nature gods" whom Zoroaster rejected returned in full strength, sometimes under new names or with different functions. For instance, "Vohu" Manah takes on the new duty of master of cattle. Such deities as Asha ("right") and Kshathra ("power") are now divinities of fire and metals, respectively. "The Amesha Spentas are female archangels or goddesses. The number of angels has greatly increased."(85).

(Z) Final Judgment

Later Zoroastrianism clarified in detail the idea of the Day of Judgment as related both to individual human beings and to the world as a whole. "Individual judgment takes place at the Chinvad Bridge. Four days after death, standing before the divine judges, the soul sees its good and evil deeds weighed in the scales. Then it passes ever the dreaded bridge. If the soul is wicked, the sharp edge of the bridge stands edgewise and gives no passage, and the soul plunges headlong to the hell". "If the soul is good", continues the learned author, "it is met by an amiable apparition (who turns out to be the soul's good deeds), who embraces it, leading it to bliss on the further side. Both the miseries of hell and the bliss of heaven are described in vivid detail"(86).

Regarding the final judgment of the world, later Zoroastrianism told a clear and detailed story. "The last three millennia are to be presided over by three Posthumous sons of Zoroaster—Oshetar, Oshetarmah, and most important of the three, Saoshyans (or Saoshyant)—who are destined to preside over the final 'renovation' of the world". "All the dead will then be resurrected, heaven and hell both being emptied of their residents for the impending great assize. In a kind of trial by ordeal, every soul will have to walk through the river of fire. To the righteous, it will seem like warm milk, but to evil it will bring unspeakable pain as it burns the evil out of them."(87)

At the end of the above-mentioned final events, Ahura Mazda and his angels will conquer "Ahriman" and his large number of evil coherts and finish them in the final fire or hell. Finally, all the survivors of these unhappy and painful events will live together in complete happiness. "In Zoroastrian metaphor, the whole universe will be made new. Even hell will be redeemed, as Ahura Mazda 'brings the land of hell back for the enlargement of the world: the renovation arises in the universe by his will, and the world is immortal forever and everlasting."(88) It may be pointed out that the above-mentioned "apocalyptic" picture has some similarity with that of the Semitic religion or tradition.

Finally, like Mahayana Buddhism, Zoroastrianism preaches a doctrine of "universal salvation". At last Ahura Mazda's power will be enforced in the rescue of all the people of the world. The similarity in the apocalyptic vision of Zoroastrianism with that of the Semitic religion is accidental in the absence of any proof of contact between them.(89)

(A1) <u>CONTEMPORARY ZOROASTRIANISM</u>

When the Muslims conquered Iran in 641 C.E., Zoroastrianism fell with the Sassanid kingdom which used it as its state religion; then in its place under the Muslim rule, Islam became the religion of the state. However, a few followers of the old religion remained but resisted conversion to Islam. The identified themselves as "<u>Zardustrian</u> (Zoroastrians) and

<u>Boh-dinan</u> ("followers of the good religion"), but to the Muslims they were Gabars("infidels")(90). It is reported that with the time of tension between the Iranians and the Muslim rulers settled, the latter realised that the formers were "people of book", and then oppression gave way to tolerance.

It should be mentioned that the Zoroastrians remained faithful to their religion even under a very difficult time beginning from the Muslim conquest of their country, mentioned above. Their priests continued to perform their duties at the fire temples, "and generations of their sons and daughters have been invested with the sacred shirt and sacred cord, symbolizing their coming of age in things religious"(91). Moreover, they also maintained their peculiar marriage and funeral customs, and their elaborate rituals of purification as well.

Some Zoroastrians fled to India and settled in Mombai where they are well-known as businessmen thus a very prosperous community. We are told that they erected their first fire temple at Sanjan in Gujarat. It was eventually moved to Udvada, where it exists until now as a well-known place of pilgrimage for Indian Zoroastrians (92).

It is interesting to take note of the fact that Zervanism, the Mithra cult and Manichaeism were branches of the original Ahura

Mazda doctrine. We can say that "Parseeism" assumed several forms and communicated several new ideas or impulses to other religions. It is known that post-biblical Judaism also was influenced in many ways by Persia, for Ahura Mazda was the only deity of the ancient world who could be equated with the God of the Bible. The religion of Zoroaster has certain doctrines in common with Judaism and Christianity: the universal last judgment, apocalypse, and individual reward or punishment (93).

Finally, since the establishment of the Islamic rule in Iran, as mentioned above, Zoroastrianism survived only in small secret underground community gatherings, but it was not completely destroyed. For example, the fire temples all over Persia continued to exist and function even though some orthodox Muslims rejected them. "Today there are still some nine thousand members of the sect, now called the Gehr. Around the year 1000 one of these clandestine Parsees, Firdusi, produced the Persian epic <u>Shah Namah</u> ("Book of the Kings"), one of the major works of world literature, which breathes the whole spirit of the Orient"(94).

CH. 1 : FOOTNOTES

1. Smith, Wilfred C. The Meaning and End of Religion, Macmillan, New York, 1963, p. 63; also cf. "Hinduism" Oxford English Dictionary, V, p. 293. The related word Hindu is of ancient and more common usage in India, though in origin it appears to be a Persian rendering of the name of the Sindh (or Indus) river and region given and used by the Muslim rulers.

2. Schoeps, Hans-Joachim, The Religions of Mankind: Their Origin and Developmen. Anchor Books, Doubleday & Company, Inc., Garden City, New York, 1968, p.158.

3. Ibid. cf. B. Allchin and R. Allchin, The Birth of Indian Civilization, Penguin, Baltimore, 1968.

4. Cf. ibid., ref. in Basham, op. cit., pp. 14-28.

5. Ibid., p. 59, ref. J. Marshall et al., Mouhenjodaro and the Indus Civilization, Oxford University Press, London, 1931, quoted from Basham, op. cit., p. 23.

6. Ibid., p. 60. For more information on the Indus Valley Civilization, cf. ibid. p. 62.

7. Linguistic evidence links them with other groups who swept off the Central Eurasian plain at about this time and

established themselves in such different countries as Iran, Greece, Rome, and Germany.

8. The most important of the Vedas is <u>Rig Veda</u>, consists of 1,028 hymns composed by some unknown seers (<u>rishis</u>), during the period of approximately 1500 to 1000 B.C. only for use in the religious rituals of the Aryans. These hymns were not written down until the fifteen and sixteenth centuries C. E. For more information about the Vedas, cf. W. Norman Brown, <u>Man in the Universe</u>: <u>Some Continuities in Indian Thought</u>, Oxford and I B H Publishing Co., Calcutta, 1966, p. 7.

9. The poems are Veda Samhita, and other elements are, respectively, <u>Veda Brahmana</u>, Veda Aranyaka and Veda Upanishad.

10. Writings which are <u>shruti</u> are different from <u>smriti</u> (which is remembered) a category which embraces traditional Indian religious classics such as the <u>Bhagavad Gita</u>, the <u>Laws of Manu</u>, and the two epics. From the Vedas is found the story of the Aryan invasion of India and the exploits and the priestly life of those invaders. Their "enemies" or more suitably the natives of India called the <u>Dasas</u> (Dravidians), dark-skinned and ill-favoured, still rich in cattle and dwelling in fortified places which have been conquered by the Aryans. The Vedas refer to this conquest as well as internal wars among the Aryans tribes.

11. Aryans were not involved for some centuries either writing or building cities. Political power or organisation centred in a chief--<u>rajah</u>, was head of the larger family. Marriage was apparently monogamous and permanent. He had no priestly tasks. His political power was limited by a council of leading persons.

12. <u>Ibid.</u>, p. 64.For more information on Aryan life and culture, cf. <u>ibid.</u>, p. 64f.

13. <u>Ibid.</u> Vedic deities were sometimes classified into three groups—of the sky, air and earth. For more information on this subject, cf. Arther B. Keith, <u>The Religion and Philosophy of the Vedas and the Upanishads</u>, I, Harard, Cambgridge Mass., 1925, ch. 8.

14. <u>Ibid.</u>, p. 163. Another popular proverb says he who has lived a good life on earth is reborn as a Brahmin or warrior, while he who lived an unworthy life must expiate for his works in the form of dog or a pig. For more information on India, cf. <u>ibid.</u>, p. 165; also cf. Brown, <u>op. cit.</u>, pp. 21ff.

15. <u>Ibid.</u>, p. 165. For more information on Varuna, Surya, Savitar, cf. <u>ibid.</u>, pp. 165f. and Rig Veda, 111. 62. 10.

16. <u>Ibid.</u>, p. 166. For more information on Vedic gods, cf. <u>ibid.</u>, pp.167.

17. <u>Ibid.</u>, p.164. For more information on this subject cf.(Hutchison, <u>op. cit.</u>,), p. 176.

18. Ibid., p. 165. For more information on this subject, cf. ibid., pp. 165f.

19. Ibid., p. 165

20. Ibid., p. 166. Following Buddhism, Shankara established monastic orders and monasteries all over India, a very bad innovation. For more information on him also cf. Hutchison, op. cit., pp. 153f.

21. Ibid., p. 167. For more information on this subject, cf. ibid., pp. 167f.; Hutchison, op.cit., p.154.

22. Ibid., p. 167; also cf. Hutchison, op. cit., pp. 76, 82, 89-94, etc.

23. Quoted in ibid., p.169.

24. Ibid., p. 169. For more information about these persons, cf. ibid., pp.169ff; Hutchison, op. cit., pp. 167f.

25. Schoeps, op. cit., p. 170; also cf. Hutchison, op. cit., p. 167.

26. Schoeps, op. cit., p.170.

27. Ibid.; also cf. Basham, A. L., The Wonder That Was India, Montreal, 1969, pp.168f; for more information on Gandhi, cf. Hutchison, op. cit., pp. 156, 168-170, 516, 517; Schoeps, op. cit., pp. 169f.

28. 28. Moore, George F., History of Religion, I, Scribner, New York, 1948, Ch. 12 ref, Hutchison, op. cit., p.81.

29. Hutchison, op. cit., p. 82.

30. Zimmer, H., Philosophies of India, Maridian Books, New York, 1957, pp. 181f.

31. Ibid., p. 183. Others were like Makhali Goshala, founder of the Ajivikas sect, which exerted considerable influence for almost a millennium in India until it finally died out in the fourteenth century. While well-known in India, the Ajivikas are little known in the west or even outside India in the East. For more information on this subject, cf. Basham, A. L., The Wonder that Was India, Grove Press, New York, 1959, pp. 294f.; Digha Nikaya, I, p. 47 f. as quoted in William T. de Bary (ed.), Sources of Indian Tradition, Columbia, New York, 1958, pp. 41ff. ; Heinrich Zimmmortal misery to the farther shore of salvation. The images of the ford and the fordfinder are strongly rooted not only in Jainism but also in Buddhism and in other Indian faiths; also cf. Schoeps, op. cit., p. 175.

32. Hutchison, op. cit., p. 84.

33. Presser, Philosophies of India, Meridian Books, New York, 1957, pp. 181f, also cf. Jaina Sutras, H. Jacobi (tr.), Sacred Books of the East, xxii, Oxford University Press, London, 1884, p. 152. By 'fordfinder' Jains have meant a great man who has discovered a way across the stream of mortal misery to the farther shore of salvation.

34. Zaehner, op. cit., p. 279.

35. Norman Brown, W., India, Pakistan, Ceylon, rev. ed., University of Pennsylvania Press, Philadelphia, 1951, p. 93;

also cf. Hutchison, op. cit., p.85. For the life of the Jaina founders cf. Hutchison, op. cit., pp.85-88.

36. Hutchison, op. cit., p. 89; also cf. de Bary, op. cit., pp. 61f.

37. de Bary, op. cit., p. 91.

38. Cf. a Jaina Sutra for tapas and ahimsa, pp. 202-210; also cf. Hutchison, op. cit., pp.90f.

39. John B. Noss, Man's Relgions, end ed., Macmillan, New York, 1963, p.163.

40. Singh, Khushwant, History of the Sikhs, I, Princeton, Princeton, N. J., 1963, p. 24; also cf. William T. de Bary(ed.), Sources of Indian Tradition, Columbia, New York, 1958, p. 532; for a comprehensive information about Kabir's role in uniting the Hinduism and Islam, cf. Hedayetullah, Muhammad, Kabir: The Apostle of Hindu-Muslim Unity, Matilal Banarsidas, Delhi, 1977.

41. Singh, op. cit., p. 31.

42. Ibid., p. 32.

43. Ibid., p. 36.

44. Selections from the Sacred Writings of the Sikhism, Trilochan Singh et. al. (trans.), G. Allen, London, 1960, p. 46.

45. de Bary, op. cit., p. 537.

46. Hutchison, op. cit., p. 179.

47. de Bary, op. cit., p. 537.

48. Singh, op. cit., p. 45.

49. Singh, K., The Sikhs Today, Orient Longmans, Calcutta, 1964, p. 5.

50. Cf. de Bary, op. cit., p. 541; also cf. Singh, K., The Sikhs Today, G. Allen, London, 1953, pp. 27f.; MacAuliffe, The Sikh Religion, ref. Noss, J. B., Man's Religions, 2nd. ed., Macmillan, New York, 1956, p. 283.

51. Singh, The Sikhs Today, op. cit., p. 29.

52. Ibid.

53. Archer, John C., The Sikhs in Relation to Hindus, Muslims, Christians and Ahmadiyyas, Princeton, N. J., 1946, p. 291.

54. Hutchison, op. cit., p. 100.

55. Cf. Warren, H. C., Buddhism in Translations, Harvard, Cambridge, Mass., 1922, p. 388; A. L. Basham, The Wonder that was India, Grove Press, New York, 1959, p. 257.

56. Cf. Warren, op. cit., pp. 60-67.

57. Hutchison, op. cit., p. 103. For more information on Buddha's life in this regard, cf. Warren, op. cit., pp. 67f.; Basham, op. cit., p. 358; Kanneth, Morgan (ed.), The Path of the Buddha, Ronald, New York, 1950, pp. 8f.; Richard Rabinson, The Buddhist Religion, Dickenson, Belmont, Calif., 1970, pp. 17f.

58. Hutchison, op. cit., p103.

59. Rabinson, op.cit., p. 18.

60. Hutchison, op. cit., p. 104.

61. Ibid.

62. Ibid., p. 105.

63. Rhys Davis, T. W., Buddhism, SPCK, London, 1903.

64. Morgan, op. cit., p. 35.

65. Warren, op. cit., p. 109.

66. Cf. Zimmer, op. cit., p. 473. Coomaraswamy has invented the term "despirated" for Nirvana, as the negative of "aspirated". For more information about Buddha's teaching, cf. Hutchison, op. cit., pp. 107ff.

67. Morgan, op. cit., p. 238.

68. Hutchison, op. cit., p. 129.

69. Chang, G. C., The Hundred Thousand Songs of Milarapa, University Books, New Hyde Park, N. Y., 1962, ref. in Hutchison, op. cit., p. 129.

70. Morgan, op. cit., p. 248. For more information about Tibbetan Buddhism, cf. Hutchison, op. cit., pp. 131f.

71. **Hutchison, op. cit., p.271; also cf. Schoeps, op. cit., p. 79.**

72. **Ibid., p. 272; also cf. Schoeps, op. cit., p. 80.**

73. **Ibid.**

74. **Ibid.**

75. **Zaehner, Robert C. The Dawn and Twilight of Zoroastrianism. Putnam, New York, 1961, pp. 25f.; also cf. John C. Archer and Carl E. Purinton, Faiths II: Live By, Ronald, New York, 1958, p. 326.**

76. For more information on Zoroaster's life, cf. Hutchison, op. cit., pp. 274ff. ; also cf. Zaehner, op. cit., pp33f. It may be mentioned here that one estimate places his life at 1500 B. C., another at 3000 B. C., and still another one at 6000 B. C. The traditional Zoroastrian estimate, endorsed by most Western or modern scholars, 628—551 B. C, accords better with existing evidence than any alternative. By the way, the important clue is the tradition which dates the founder "258 years before Alexander", that is , before Alexader's sack of Persepolis in 330 B. C. This would be 588 B. C. , presumably the date of Zoroaster's conversion of King Vishtaspa, which was the turning point of Zoroaster's career. If this is right, Zoroaster was a contemporary of Buddha, Confucius, Laotzu as well as of the prophets of Israel and others of that time. It may be pointed out that if this chronology is right, Zoroaster's life followed that of the Prophet Moses by some six hundred years (cf. 6000 B. C. is the estimate of J. M. Ranina in The Essential Principles of Zoroastrianism, P. D. Clinoy, Bombay, 1961, p. 3.

77. Hutchison, op. cit., p. 276.

78. J. Duchesne-Guillemin, The Hymns of Zoroastra, J. Murray, London, 1952,

pp. 65f.

79. Hutchison, op. cit., p. 277.

80. Ibid., p. 279.

81. Ibid.,p. 280.

82. Ballou, R. O., The Bible of the World. Viking, New York, 1947, p. 606.

83. Hutchison, op. cit., p. 282.

84. Schoeps, Hans-Joachim, op. cit. p. 85.

85. Hutchison, op. cit., p. 283.

86. Ibid., p. 284.

87. Ibid.

88. Ballou, op, cit., p. 634.

89. Cf. Hutchison, op. cit., p. 285.

90. Ibid.

91. Ibid.

92. Ibid., p. 286.

93. Schoeps, op. cit., p. 93.

94. Ibid., p. 94.

CH. 2: CHINESE RELIGION: BUDDHISM

Historically, since the first century (61 C.E.) on, Mahayana Buddhism with its established doctrine of the Bodhisattvas (body or being of enlightenment or wisdom) continuously entered into China, and, curiously, entered into alliance with native systems of doctrine. Under Buddhist influence, new schools of religion were established, and by the sixth century had officially become the state religion. We are told "that the Chinese Buddhists created their own canon of religious scriptures, seven hundred times more voluminous than the Bible."(1) This very large literature is probably responsible for the creation of as many as ten different Buddhist sects in China. But among the common people, only the very practical "School of Meditation" (Chan-tsung) and the

"School of the Pure Land"(Tsing-tu) have been successful. We are also told that the Buddhism of the "School of the Pure Land" became a religion of personal salvation; it sought salvation in the heavenly Buddha's paradise where his devotees would be received after death. "The Nirvana doctrine of the primitive Buddhist communities plays scarcely any part in Amitabha Buddism"(2)

We are also told that the Buddha Amitabha is shown in many temple images as extremely majestic and kind. By and large, he is shown enthroned on a lotus, or otherwise standing tall holding a lotus flower in one hand. It is also reported that the Buddhism of the 'School of the Pure Land' is on the way to becoming a religion of grace; personal salvation is sought in the heavenly Buddha's paradise, into which his devotees will be received after death.

The notable religious figures of ancient China were Confucius (551-479 B.C.E.) and Lao-tzu (604--B.C.).As humans, they demonstrated what is called ultimate concern of valuation. What is unique about Confucius (Kung-tse) and the tradition to which he gave conclusive expression is that the object of ultimate concern was Chinese society itself. In other words, the distinctive religious response is in Confucius, reflected back to society itself. Although this attitude was generated in very ancient times, it became explicit and conscious in the life and thought of Confucius.

The Chan school begins from the legend that the Buddha (Fo in Chinese): one day instead of explaining his doctrine, he showed his audience a golden flower with a smile. A beginner monk understood it and he smiled back. That means that the mystery lies not in his words, but in deep meditation on the flower itself.

It may be pointed out that China stands, after India, as the oldest civilized tradition of the world. (Before the 6th century B. C. there was the Chou dynasty which was in power in 1120 B.C.E., but even before that there was the Shang, which had reigned from 1800 B.C.E. to 1120 B.C.E., and before the Shang was the pre-historic Hsia dynasty with its sage kings, Yao and Shun).

Relating to the religio-political history, the Chou dynasty was displaced by the Ch'in in 221 B.C.E. which was succeeded by the Han during whose time Confucianism was given the role of the established faith or philosophy which lasted until 1911 C.E.

As for the Buddhist schools, the Tsing school is the most popular and widespread. It is stated that before the Chinese revolution (1911) sixty percent of the Chinese Buddhists belonged to it. The "Pure Land", "also called the 'great western paradise,' is the heaven in which Buddha Amitaba, the Buddha Immeasurable Radiance, sits enthroned."(3)

Amitabhha is the heavenly counterpart of the historical Buddha (Dhyanibuddha)—a divine Buddha of pure honour who rules as master of paradise or eternal light and saves the believers. For most people who do not want to be an arhat, it is enough for them to worship the Buddha Amitaba, the "heavenly helper of believers" who could be just ordinary people instead of good workers or ascetics. In other words, neither good work nor asceticism is needed for them.

To end this discussion, we are told: "The Buddhism of the 'School of the Pure Land' is on the way to becoming a religion of grace; personal salvation is sought in the heavenly Buddha's paradise, into which his devotees will be received after death. The Nirvana doctrine of the primitive Buddhist Communities plays scarcely any part in Amitaba Buddhism"(4).

Finally, "By the ninth century Buddhism had made its decisive contribution to China. Some aspects of the new faith, like cremation and asceticism, China rejected; other aspects, such as a more active philanthropy and a new philosophic impetus, were accepted. Yet perhaps Buddhism's greatest contribution to the Chinese tradition was the stimulus it provided for the new-Confucian revival which followed."(5)

Lao-Tse and the Tao-Te-King

Chinese religious conjecture reached its peak in the work of Lao-tse ("The Old Philosopher").(6) He wrote a book entitled Tao-te-King (never translated into any other languages). It primarily deals "in ecstatic metaphysical language with Tao and Te". But indistinctness begins immediately as to what Tao and Te are? As we can see, both are very ambiguous or obscure words that have no parallels in any modern languages. "Tao means something like 'ground of being', 'way' or 'orbit'—the orbit in which the universe moves, Te means approximately 'good conduct' or 'virtue'. Tao-Te-King is thus the path of virtue, or the universal law and its effects; it is also Lao-tse's prescription of how man ought to live."(7).

Hu Shih, a modern historian, has suggested that Confucius was a Ju (court intellectual) of an ancient traditional type which has gone out of fashion and which Confucius succeeded in reviving in his own time.(8)

Confucian Themes

There are eight principal themes in the teaching of the great philosopher-mystic. The most basic is <u>Li</u> ("propriety," "courtesy," "rites and ceremonies," and "decorum"). The <u>Li chi</u> quotes Confucius as asserting that "<u>Li</u> ...is the principle by which the ancient kings embodied the laws of heaven, and regulated the expressions of human nature. Therefore, he who has attained <u>Li</u> lives and he who has lost it dies.... <u>Li</u> is based on heaven, patterned on earth, deals with the worship of the spirit and is extended to the rites and ceremonies of funerals, sacrifices to ancestors, archery, carriage driving, capping, marriage, and court audience or exchange of diplomatic visits. Therefore the sage shows the people this principle of a rationalized social order and through it everything becomes right in the family, the state and the world."(9)

However, some say emphatically that to understand Lao-tse's doctrine is to have a correct understanding of the word <u>Tao.</u> To begin with, what does it mean? Lao-tse explains in his book: "The standard of man is the earth, the standard of the earth is heaven, the standard of heaven is Tao, the standard of Tao—its own life" (10). In explaining the above-mentioned statement of Lao-tse, we cannot say that this inherent force does anything—that would be typifying it too much. Nonetheless, everything is done by Tao. "Tao is eternally without action, and yet there is nothing that it does not do. Rather, the non-doing of all beings helps it to do what it does. By <u>Wu-Wei</u> (doing nothing) and <u>puh- yen</u> (saying nothing), the condition of <u>hu- wu</u> (equilibrium) is attained. <u>We-Wei,</u> then, is having effect without acting. .Water is a symbol of the Tao; it does not contend, it takes the lowest place, and yet it is the most important thing. Tao is amoral; Lao-tse regards positive moral teachings as a symptom of degeneracy. Everything happens of its own accord; no effort is needed, for action only impairs concentrated sanctity. If the great Tao decays, then humanitarianism and justice, prudence and cleverness arise; and from these stem hypocrisy and ever multiplying conflicts among men."(11)

We are also told that there is good harmony of the universe in which humans take part by their practice of <u>li</u>. Alternately, the "pervasive" and agreeable order of the universe finds example and application in human life in a person's practice of good form.

It is reported that the ethics of Lao-tse are totally negative. It is originated in a quietist mysticism which ascribes no particular place to man in this whole world of existence. The object is to free man from getting involved and let him go back into the ultimate motive or position—Tao. But for actual knowledge of Tao, neither conjecturing nor learning is needed nor actual worldly wisdom such as Confucius taught.

Thus, Lao-tse says, "Without looking out of the window, one sees the course of heaven. Without going out of the house, one knows the world. The farther one goes away, the less one perceives. Therefore, the wise man knows without stirring, gives names to things without seeing them, and completes without acting"(12). Thus, in fact, Lao-tse draws near ancient Buddhism in these teachings. In other words, not to act, not to interfere in the natural course of events, is man's duty. Some interesting conclusions draw from this principle which are "expressed in the Tao-te-king."(13)

On the other hand, we are told that following the Chinese tradition or virtue of respect for one's father in particular and for elders in general, Confucius gave open expression and unconditional support to filial piety (hsia) even to the extent of defending and hiding a father's crime from the government.

For example, the "Duke of She" observed Confucius: "Among us there was an upright man called Kung who was so upright that when his father appropriated a sheep, he bore witness against him". Confucius said the upright men among us are not like that. A father will screen his son and a son his father—yet uprightness is to be found in that" ("Analects" x111, 18.ref. Hutchison, p.197. (Filial piety consisted of an inward respect for one's parents and all elders). A significant application of the virtue of filial piety to Chinese society lay in the traditional five great relations. In the Li Chi's "formula"; they are the following:

1. Kindness in the father, filial piety in the son.
2. Gentility in the elder brother, humanity and respect in the younger.
3. Righteous behaviour in the husband, obedience in the wife.
4. Humane consideration in elders, defense in juniors.
5. Benevolence in rulers, loyalty in ministers and subjects.(14)

It should be emphasised here that in general, the Li Chi's "formula" provided the moral foundation for Confucius's humanistic ideal, which included also excellence of all sorts.

Further more, Shu Jen is fulfilled in the closely related quality of shu, which is perhaps best translated as "reciprocity". When asked, "Is there any one word that can serve as a principle for the conduct of life"? Confucius said: "Perhaps the word reciprocity": Do not do to others what you would not want others to do to you."(15)

The Doctrine of Confucius

Confucius (Kung-tse) was like Lao-tse since he too did not consider himself as the agent of a divine power. But unlike the latter, he was a more seriousminded political figure, whose criticisms of the conditions of his society were motivated by a practical longing to improve it.

Confucius traveled among a few princely courts, and was active as a political adviser. Leaving aside the legendary stories of his life, it is enough to say that he preached his teachings in words and living examples which were written down long after his death (479 B.C). His disciples formed a school of Scribes. The school produced the <u>Annals of Spring and Autum</u>, a book of moral and political wisdom for princes, and the <u>Book of Historical</u> <u>Documents,</u> an abridgement of ancient Chinese institutions and customs. More important than these writings is the <u>Lun Yii</u>, "Discourses and dialogues", written by the third generation of his disciples, preserving recollections of the master (Confucius) and some of his sayings.(16)

Confucius thought of the Tao in its moral and social aspects in connection with right government of a state. The political basis of his thinking is clear; his mind focused mainly on the ideas of a nation and rule. "Within society, the Tao operates in two forms: in music and in the <u>li</u>, the ritual rules for community life. There are mysterious powers that influence and govern social life. Morality governs behavior, beautiful music governs feeling."(17) Since the production of these powers usually produce political disturbance, they have to be controlled and regulated by the emperor who is the authority and protector of law and order. The ruler is the head of the state, and because Tao is specially concentrated in him, he is also the head of the state religion, its main priest. Above him, as the preserver of his throne, there is only heaven, whose son he is.

Confucius thinks rites (li) is extremely important for the nation. For example, a people held in discipline only by the threats of punishment would lose its moral sense and deteriorate, while a people guided by moral principle would have a sense of moral obligation and work hard for well-being. "In the LunYu Confucius is reported to have said: "The superior man makes honesty the foundation of his existence. He uses it with address and consideration. He speaks of it with modesty, and carries it out with seniority and faithfulness. Truly, this is the superior man."(18)

As for the religious elements in Confucianism, some Chinese scholars think that Confucius' teachings constitute an ethical philosophy rather than a religion.

Of course, if we think of the Semitic religions, Confucianism is certainly not a religion, but a moral philosophy.

"Yet in the broader sense of a distinctive system of holy forms which provide orientation for human life, Confucianism comes within the bounds of religion."(19). Whether or not Confucius' teachings constitute a religion or philosophy? We are told, Confucius' outlook was summed up precisely in his own maxim: "To devote oneself earnestly to one's duty to humanity and while respecting the spirits to stay aloof from them may be called wisdom."(20).

However, at least three religious elements may be pointed out in Confucius' teaching: First, was his love of ritual. "His disciple Tzu kung questioned the ritual sacrifice of sheep, to which Confucius replied: "You love the sheep and I love the ceremony" (21). Lin Yutang has remarked of this expression of Confucius' teachings by saying that if he were a Christian, he would have become an important "Churchman."(22).

A second religious element was Confucius' sense of historical meaning which located the archetypal good age in the past and sought to this idealised past: "With diffrent symbols, this glorification of an ideal past has been a recurring attitude in many religions."(23).

In the process of thinking of Confucius, the ideal age of the past was the early days of the Chou dynasty. In addition to the above, the most unmistakable religious element in Confucius' thought was his sense of profession and mission, "his sense of being <u>called</u> and <u>sent</u>". This attitude, is of course, a principal sign of actual religious experience wherever it happens. In Confucius' life, it was "Heaven" that called him and sent him back, as he believed."Moreover, this belief constituted the meaning of his life. Especially during his years of wandering and rejection, this mission sustained him. Hence despite his agnosticism and his scorn of popular religion or superstition, Confucius was in this sense a religious person."(24).

In other words, Confucius does not seek release; the most he wants to be protected from cultural disorder or chaos. He wants as the reward of moral goodness or work long healthy and wealthy life, and after death the protection of a good name. Ethics has no supernatural meaning. An educated Chinese refuses to consider himself permanently affected by sin. Wrong doing consists of offenses against seniors like parents, ancestors, superiors at the official level, or else violating traditional ceremonies or social obligations.

It should be stated here emphatically that the basis of the Chinese society is the family; the continuing factor in life is the religious respect that is practiced or observed according to a fixed ceremonials also, Confucius willingly restored the Chinese national ancestor cult. Thus, Confucius said, "To honour the dead as if they are still living", "is, according to Confucius, "an expression of supreme Childlike submissiveness. To have no son who can continue the ancestor cult is regarded as a grave offense against the family". "There is no greater sign of respect for the father than to consider him as equal to heaven". Confucius is reported to have commented in one of his discourses: "He sacrificed to his ancestors as if they were present; he sacrificed to the gods as if the gods were present. The master said: To me, sacrificing without the sense of presence is as good as not sacrificing."(25).

To conclude the present subject, let us say that Confucianism is no religion by any definition of religion but rather a rationalistic ethics based on confidence in the ultimate well-being of humanity. Naturally, Confucian philosophy is a simple common sense; Confucian ethics is a regular morality that has pervaded the whole of Chinese life and established an ideal of perfection simply within the capacity of the average man. Only because the Chinese give little recognition to religion and metaphysics, Confucius fulfilled their needs.

New Confucianism

During the centuries of Buddhist dominance in China, Confucianism was never out of the scene but only moved to the background. From this convenient "position in T'ang and Sung times", Confucianism started a "counteroffensive against Buddhism and neo-Taoism to regain its former position of dominance. The first stirrings of neo-Confucianism in the T'ang dynasty may be observed in that staunch old classicist, man of letters, and astringent critic of Buddhism, Han Yu (786-836). In his essay entitled "what is the True Way"? (Yuan tao), Han vigorously attacked both Buddhism and Taoism as unfilial, unsocial, and escapist."(26).

Han concentrated his attack on Buddhism, which was still spreading in China. His memorial on the Bone of Buddha was a bitter protest to the emperor against the honour which was being shown to a relic of Buddha. "Most of all, the emperor should not give aid and comfort by participating in these ceremonies! Rather let him give the order to seize its bone and have it cast into the fire. As for the Buddhists, they are a degenerate and immoral lot, with their ascetic practices and their superstitious ritual around this stinking bone!"(27).

In the Sung dynasty, neo-Confucianism became a movement heavily influential both in politics and philosophy. In many instances, philosophers were advisers to emperors and other government officials.

Sung neo-Confucianism began with the Chou Tun-yi (1017-1073). Chou was heavily influenced by Taoism. It is reported that his philosophic idea of the Ultimate was given to him in a drawing by a Taoist priest. His ethic of serene and "having no desire" depicts a similar influence. Whatever his sources, Chou's writing elaborately explained a cosmology in which all things come from the "great ultimate (t'ai chi)". This word and idea may be found in the Han dynasty "Great Appendix" to the "Book of Changes"(28).

Rise of Taoism (Lao Tzu and Chuang Tzu)

Like Confucianism, Taoism began in the Chou period. Some scholars doubt whether the Tao Te Ching ("Classic of the Way and Its Power") could possibly have been written by Lao Tzu, an older contemporary of Confucius. Yes, he is.(29)

The Tao Te Ching, is a short mysterious poem, divided into sixty-five to eighty-one stanzas (there are two opinions about it), translated into English many times.

The principal term of the Tao te Ching is, of course, Tao (Way). Confucius used it to characterize the social system and Way which he advocated and which he believed to be in accord with heaven and earth.

Themes of the Tao Te Ching

The Taoists gave their own special mystical interpretation to the idea of Tao. Still the doctrine of Lao-tse has gone through a developmental process, as usual. It has developed into a religion, called Taoism, because eventually it developed a practical ethics and a regular priestly organisation. As a result, "the antiworldly rationalistic doctrine of the aristocratic mystic Lao-tse has merged with the age-old Chinese profession of magi (tao-shi)."(30).

Apart from this, the hermits joined forces to constitute monastic communities. However, Monastic Taoism performed without any influence on people's life because its strong mystic efforts made it avoid the world. That means, it was never fully understood by the Chinese people in general. In order to overcome this problem, they undertook the following measures: thus one recurring suggestion is to call it "the one" since from the Tao comes one. Another is to designate it by paradox and negation:

We look at it and do not see it;
Its name is The Invisible.
We listen to it and do not hear it;
Its name is the Inaudible.
We touch it and do no find it,
Its name is The Subtle (formless).
These three cannot be further inquired into.

And hence merge into one.

Going up high it is not bright, and coming down
    low, it is not dark.
    Infinite and boundless, it cannot be given
    any name;

It reverts to nothingness.(31)

Other symbols for the Tao appear from study of the Tao te teaching, particularly water, "the female, the uncarved block, the valley, the void, and the infant. All especially are, in terms of Chinese tradition, yin and not yang". The Tao te ching says:

The best (man) is like water,
Water is good; it benefits all things
    and does not compete with them
It dwells in (lowly) places that all disdain.
This is why it is so near to Tao.
The spirit of the valley never dies.
    it is called the subtle and profound female.
The gate of the subtle and profound female
    is the root of Heaven and Earth.(32).

Soon the Taoiost magicians were exercising their non-religious power almost in every field of Chinese life. For example, they started selling amulets, practised exorcism of demons, alchemy and soothsaying. It is said that by "borrowings from the ancestor cult, the whole cosmos was peopled with nature gods and local deities"(33). They had some special gods for different occupations. "Thus students venerated Wan-Chang, the disembodied spirit of an official of the Chow dynasty, as the god of literature—who thereafter frequently appeared in person to famous scholars. Merchants venerated the war god Kvan–ti, a successful soldier of fortune of the Han dynasty"(34).

At this stage, it should be stated emphatically that despite what is stated above, we can also see in the stanzas below the plea for a simple and natural way. Thus, Taoist morality is sometimes defined "one of inaction". The Chinese term <u>Wu Wei</u> means "inaction" or action without action". Some of the texts, considered literally, means exactly that. For instance, "Therefore the sage manages affairs without action....(35). Commenting on the above statement, Hutchison says, "Nevertheless, in context the meaning seems to be one of cooperating with the Tao. Just as a swimmer makes better progress by swimming with the waves than by fighting them, so a person should swim with the wave of Tao. One should thus do what is natural, namely, cooperate with the Tao."(36).

Taoist Ethics

Before we proceed further, let us say a few words on Taoist ethics. Taoist ethics emphasised the way of natural simplicity and nature's harmony. Like most of the Chou schools, it was anti-militarist and had a strong feeling of the evil of war, and also of the harsh or forcible compulsion process of the government. Taoism was committed to a "laissez-faire" view of government. "Ruling a big country is like cooking a small fish", which means, "too much handling spoils it, asserted the Tao te ching."(37)

In the long run, Taoism organised a complex hierarchical organisation of priests, monks and up to a Pope. The priests assumed the functions of soothsayers and magicians. They also performed some social functions like purging streets, houses and persons of evil characters.

In 666 C.E. Lao-tse was officially "deified" during the Tang dynasty (7th--9th centuries), Taoism reached the climax of its sway among the people and of the official level. Eventually, we are told, it rapidly fallen away "into a superstation of the lower classes", and became only a "system of exorcism". "The Tao was viewed as a mysterious magical force men could acquire for themselves."(38). By using this force, they believed, they could, for instance, prolong their lives. "The first Taoist pope, Chang Tao-ling, was reputed to have an elixir that conferred immortality.

To this day, his descendants reside on the Dragon-tiger Mountain, where Chang Tao-ling, strengthened by his elixir, rose into the air and vanished."(39).

By and large, it may be stated that the real form that Taoism has taken is nothing more than the continuation of ancient Chinese folk religion. As regular religion, Taoism has more or less disappeared in China, There are only a few Taoist monasteries left in the whole country. Its spirits and gods have gone to the fold of folk religion, and its philosophical ideas have been taken over by Buddhism, one of the oldest religions of the East.

The developmental history of Confucianism has taken a different course. According to historical evidence, from 57 B.C. to 1911, with some breaks, it was the state religion of China. However, irrespective of the official status for this religion, the real teachings of the founder had little in practice. Thus we are told, "By imperial edict of A.D. 267, an ox had to be sacrificed to Confucius four times a year. In A.D. 555 it was ordered that a Confucian temple be established in every prefectural city, so that the whole country was covered with sanctuaries in honour of the sage. But this cult of the deified philosopher, celebrated with animal sacrifices in ornate temples, to the accompaniment of music, had very little to do with the simple, pure teachings of Kung-tse. Against his wishes, he became the founder of a religion which followed its own laws and had its own history, with numerous triumphs and setbacks, until at last the writings of Confucius and his successors became the accepted code of orthodoxy in politics, morality and faith."(40).

Finally, the Confucian state religion was a combination of ancestor cult, nature worship, astrology and the founder's morality. It served the purposes of a centrally –controlled state in which the emperor, as the "Son of Heaven" and chief of the religion, dedicated to his "symbolic" ancestor, Confucius, in the largest temple of the empire, the "Temple of Heaven", near Peking. We are told that this temple stood for thousands of years as the largest religious monument in history. The rules administering the ceremonies were slowly developed into a scholarly system, and a hard-line Confucian creed eventually was expended.

In 1905 the revolutionary regime abolished the old Confucian style examinations and a modern system of schooling was established in China. The declaration of the republic in 1911 "transformed" China into a modern nation-state. "Deposition of the 'Son of Heaven' was a blow to the very heart of Confucianism, which since then ceased to exist as a theocratic political system. The Temple of Heaven near Peking was made into a vast park for the common people."(41).

Notwithstanding all the events leading up to the revolution and following it, it appears that the Chinese people do not seem to have abandoned their religious tradition altogether. For instance, Dr. Sun Yat-sen, "the father of the Chinese Revolution", called his people to remember the ethical values implied in the teachings of the sages when they begun organising their new society when our country is full with traitors, Communists and lax in morals it proves that we have abandoned these virtues. If we want to rescue our national identity, we must cultivate these virtues afresh and make them the foundation stones "of a new life"(42).

The optimists believed that the principal attitudes of thought and emotion in individual Chinese will continue to be Confucian long after the old teachings have been officially cancelled. We are told that this is happening at present in the Chinese People's Republic—that ancient religious ideas have merged with the official government ideology of "Marxism-Leninism". The doctrine of Confucius is not under attack as "feudalistic" and harmful to the building of socialism. Almost all the Confucian temples in today's China have been selected for secular purposes. The Chiang Kai-shek government of Taiwan, on the other hand, declared the birthday of Confucius an official holiday to be celebrated annually. Notwithstanding the "Bolshevization" of the Chinese mainland, the basic thinking of the individual Chinese still appears "more Confucius than Marxist".(43).

Religion in Japan: Buddhism

At the outset, it should be mentioned that the formal introduction of Buddhism into Japan is particularly dated as 538 or 552 of C. E. when the Japanese government received the detailed information about this foreign religion. During the following centuries, Japan came under the influence of both China and Korea where Buddhism had been thriving. In Japan, Buddhism **inclined to absorb the ways or characters** of the natives and to enter into an alliance with their religion—Shintoism but not fully merging with it, for the former was not compatible with the latter which has also developed earthly matters. However, some adaptation did take place, e.g., sooth-saying and the sale of amulets were integrated with the Japanese Buddhism. Furthermore, the element of "sectarianism" or division of Shintoism also eventually developed in Buddhism.

Notwithstanding the history of Japan is much later than those of China and India, yet the Japanese have imparted their own distinctive character to all the materials that have come to their land from the Asian mainland and more recently from the West. "Illustration of this process of assimilation and transformation range from language and art to virtually every other significant element of Japanese culture. However, there is no more important example than Japanese Buddhism, which is surely as much Japanese as it is Buddhist"(44). It may be mentioned here that like some other cultures, in Japan nature and society together constitute the object of ultimate concern. This fact is found in their religious life as well, as we will see later. H. Nakamura confirmed this fact when he says the Japanese apprehend the "absolute in the phenomenal world"(45).

The formal introduction of Buddhism into Japan is dated as 538 or 552 of C. E. when the Japanese government received the detailed information about this foreign religion. It may be mentioned, that during the following centuries, Japan had been under the influence of both China and Korea, where Buddhism had been thriving. Interestingly, in Japan Buddhism inclined to adopt the way of the natives and to enter into an alliance with their religion—Shintoism, but not fully merging with it for the former was not compatible with the latter which is also devoted to earthly matters. However, some adaptation did take place, for example, sooth saying and the sale to amulets integrated with the Japanese Buddhism. Furthermore, the element of sectarian division of Shintoism also developed in Buddhism.

It may be mentioned here that although the Japanese tradition imported from China some elements like the Confucian ethic and emperor-worship, yet Nakamura emphatically spoke of the importance in Japan of the "concrete social nexus", " the actual social context of the individual in family, community and nation"(46).Connected with this context has been the flexibility and practicality of individuals in filling themselves into the present situation and living as a part of this actual social situation. Nakamura spoke of this situation as the Japanese 'acceptance of actuality'(47).

The different branches of Buddhism such as the Shojo (the Small Vehicle), Daijo (the Great Vehicle) and the Diamond Vehicle played a role in Japan. However, the most remarkable development is the Japanese trasformation of the Amitabha Buddha into Amida Butsu. The "true Sect of the Pure Land", founded by Shinran Shonin (at the beginning of the thirteenth century C.E.), similar to the Chinese school discussed before. It developed following the Honen Shonin's Jodo school (founded in 1175), which presently is one of the main religions of Japan with over thirteen million followers and eight thousand temples all over Japan. But Shinran's sect gained widest popularity by discarding asceticism, celibacy and monastic life, and preaching equal religious rights for women. It is reported that Shinran is compared with Martin Luther, for the former also pleaded for a religion of "pure grace and proclaimed that Amida Butsu would save wicked as well as the good, and that he conferred faith in him as a pure gift"(47A).

There is another sect known as the "sect of the Flower of the Law" established by the reformer Nichiren in 1253 C.E. It is based on a boundlessly scattered popular book of tales of Mahayana Buddhism relating to the "Lotus of the Good Law". In this book, the Buddha is made as a "supernatural saviour deity". A sect especially accepted by the "sammurai, the Japanese warrior class", it is well known for its unusual intolerance towards other Buddhist sects, "strong Japanese nationalism, and an apocalyptic, prophetic tone" which is far away from the impersonal kindness of Gautama Buddha.

The magical Bodhisattva cult of Tibetan Tantrism has developed a usual Japanese form in the Shingon group. Like the Tendai group, which promoted an esoteric philosophy, it was founded in Kyoto in the ninth century C. E. and spread quickly among the higher class during early Middle Ages. Both cults have absorbed strong compounds of mysticism but stayed within the boundary of the "Diamond Vehicle". Finally, the sectarian forms of the "Small Vehicle" has disappeared from contemporary Japan(48).

Zen Buddhism is a religion of strict self-discipline and meditation which has influenced Japanese art e. g. watercolouring, but it has also greatly influenced the Japanese army. For example, the samurai found Zen's discipline, and contempt for death the ideals they needed. The life-style practised by Zen has formed the simplest or easiest daily works, "such as the ceremony of tea-drinking, garden culture, archery, sitting postures, breathing rhythms, and so on. The aim of Zen is to disclose to the meditative person the religious significance of everyday acts, so that he will become capable of harmony with the ground of being"(49).

Shintoism

Shintoism (Path of the gods or way of the Sublime) is the national religion of Japan, of Japanese origin, without any outside influence or elements. By the way, it has no founder, no dogmatic scriptures and being a practical religion concerning matters of this world, it focuses only on family and the national matters as a whole. "The Japanese soul and the principles behind Japanese government are most authentically revealed in the Shintoist creed, especially the disposition of the individual to take his place within his clan and within the community of his nation."(50).

Like other religions, Shintoism has different periods of its development up to the present time:the first, extends to the introduction of Buddhism. "The second from 538 or 552 to 1868, when Shintoism and Buddhism mixed, and the third from 1868, when the reformed Shintoism became the state religion"(51). The oldest period had no scriptures, for the Japanese had no script before the introduction of Chinese characters (fifth to seventh centuries). Interestingly, all rules including the rituals recited at sacrifices and the supernatural story of the grandson of the sun goddess who came down upon the island of Kyushu to run the country, were passed orally.

Since the fourth century C.E. the Tenno ("Son of Heaven") or Mikado ("High Portal") held the same position in Japanese religious life until 1945 when MacArthur stripped him of his holy position.

Like other religions, Shinto has its special myth and ritual. It is also the distinctive group of values which is the human substance of what is recited in the myth and practiced in the ritual. This is called "the Japanese way of life". Shinto is the best and clearest example of practical or living religion of man—"nature-culture religion", as well-known.

Shinto also concerns itself with the fundamental question, "What is religion"? It would like to include some events which in other religions are not included in the concept and practice of religion.

Shinto Mythology

At the outset, it should be stated that to study Shinto, there are no documents parallel to other religious systems, but there are "sacred writings", especially the <u>Kojiki</u> (712 C.E. "Record of Ancient Tales"), and the <u>Nihongi</u> or <u>Nihonshoki</u> or Chronicles of Japan(720 C.E). Together, they contain the principal mythological sources of Shinto(52).

Shintoism is said to be a real Japanese national religion without any foreign influence. Naturally, it differs from most other religions in having no founder, no dogmatic scriptures, a pure religion of this world, dealing primarily with family and national community. Thus, "The Japanese soul and the principles behind Japanese government are most authentically revealed in the Shintoist creed, especially the disposition of the individual to take his place within his clan and within the community of his nation"(53).

Shinto Ritual

It is important to know that the Shinto Ritual may be described as the realisation in symbolic actions of these same values. "Shinto ritual like the myth is of diverse origins and combines a wide variety of interests. Elements of animism, fertility worship, ancestors and heroes, and nature worship are only a few of its ingredients. The sun-goddess herself combines in her own person many roles. She is the chief deity of Japan and of the imperial house as well as sun goddess."(54).

Shinto rite and myth display a spectacular local diversity. Local shrines and ceremonies have always played a particular part in Shinto. For example, "every deceased person could become a Kami ('supernatural being'),that is, the embodiment of a family's vital force, and as such eternally present."(55). By the way, this idea is the basis or the origin of the ancestor cult, characteristic of Japan and China. The Kami is worshiped on important days.

Although Shinto ritual has changed along with other things known to the society, there has not been any drastic reduction or even changes in its long history. "Contemporary Shinto ritual thus provides a point of living relations between twentieth-century Japan and its ancient past."(56).Certainly, this idea is the root of the ancestor cult, and the Kami is worshiped on important memorial days with prayers and sacrifices. But state cult, (that is the government is matsuri-goto= "religious affairs") comes before the private ancestor cult. Thus the deity of submission to the emperor, "the highest sacral power", stands higher than duty towards ancestors, for which fact, Shintoism has also been called Tennoism.

Since the beginning of the custom of offering prayers to deceased emperors in the ninth century C.E., the number of emperors officially "worshipped as gods after death" is said to be small; "of 122, there are only 12 such emperors and 3 empresses", up to 1912. Of the non-royalties who received ritual honours as gods, there were some war heroes and scholars who won national popularity such as Sugahare Michizane, who was given the "ritual honours as god of calligraphy and scholarship"(57).

It should be stated here that in Shinto folk religion, sacred animals such as the fox also play some role, as evidenced from images in Shinto shrines, but there is no evidence of totemism even in the oldest forms of Shintoism. Shinto worship has usually consisted of two aspects: attendance and offering. Offerings in ancient times consisted of such things as "first fruits, first catch of fish, or booty of war brought as food for the Kami". Offerings also consisted of prayers which are "punctuated by a clapping of hands" to draw the Kami's attention. "Many of the ritual prayers and liturgies preserved from early times show a simple and archaic beauty of language which is characteristic of Shinto"(58).

Before concluding Shintoism, let us say a few words concerning Shinto's practice of deification of natural forces which still is a living faith. The sun goddess Amaterasu is the first, as mentioned earlier. Originally thought as the material sun, "she became a spirit, the ancestral mother of the human emperor, and holds the central position in the Japanese nature cult—the sun's disk may also be seen on the national flag...." From the ancient time, "every new emperor presents himself to her... at the time of his accession". At the present time, "Japanese farmers and city dwellers" will go out of their homes in the morning "to bow toward the East, clap their hands several times and wish themselves good fortune for the new day(59).

Japan has no longer Shinto's moon cult, but it has a storm and sea god (Susanowo, "the Rager"), as well as numerous river gods and sea nymphs who use crocodiles and sharks as their messengers. There also is a harmful god of fire who causes destructive fire. Amulets and talismans are generally used for protection against these. Several holy wells, springs and mountain peaks are also worshiped in Japan. Since the country is vulnerable to earthquakes, the earthquake god is represented as a huge "fish who lies under the surface of the earth and creates quakes by moving his scales"(60). According to a catalogue of Japanese myths and gods made in 1901, there are as many as "3,132" gods.

Finally, Shinto priests have a hereditary priestly office, yet they do not constitute a class different from the public. The priests are the caretakers or protectors of the Shinto shrines, which are hierarchically ranked. There also are priestesses and religious or holy dancing girls (maikos) in all large temples.

SHINTO TODAY

It should be stated here that revival of a new Shintoism without any connection with Buddhism, began in the eighteenth century with a number of sects or divisions; some of them are founded on models borrowed from the Chinese Confucian models. There are now as many as thirteen such sects strongly based in the lower classes of the society. They seem, however, to be lacking in emotional force and ideas. "This folk Shinto seems to be an answer to the fact that official Shinto, with its rites and ceremonies in palace and shrines, has been long isolated from the people. The sects owe their great success to the touching naivete of the Japanese masses, and to all sorts of dubious practices, such as pray er-healing"(61).

To conclude the present subject, we find it appropriate to use the following statement: "In spite of officially proclaimed religious freedom, the bond between Shintoism and the people seems to have become no looser than the relationship toward the Tenno. Both still represent the real content of Japanese nationalism. An imperial house that has reigned for some seventeen hundred years has another quality from the innumerable dynasties in the rest of the world. Perhaps Japan is the only country on earth in which sacred kingship has defied all the disintegrating tendencies of Western thought. In the eyes of millions of Japanese to this day Emperor Hirohito [and his son as well] is a descendant of the sun goddess Amaterasu, and thus an 'incarnate supernatural being'. In the immediate postwar era, state Shintoism seemed doomed. But since Japan has regained her sovereignty, its star is once more in the ascendant"(62).

CH. 2: FOOTNOTES

1. Schoeps, Hans-Joachim, The Religions of Mankind: The Origin and Development, (translated from the German by Richard and Clara Winston), Anchor Books, Doubleday & Company, Inc., Garden City, New York, 1968, p.193 ; also cf. Hutchison, John A., Paths of Faith, Third Edition, McGraw-Hill Book Company, Montreal, 1969, pp. 216ff.

2. Schoeps, op. cit., p. 195; also cf. Hutchison, op. cit., p. 219.

3. Ibid., p. 194.

4. Ibid., p. 195.

5. Hutchison, op. cit., p. 223.

6. Schoeps, op. cit., p. 197; also cf. Fung, Yu-Lan, A Short History of Chinese Philosophy, Macmillan, New York, 1960, p. 283.

7. Ibid., p. 198.

8. Wing-Tsil Chan, Religious Trends in Modern China, Columbia, New York, 1953, pp. 25f.; also cf. Hutchison, op. cit., pp. 195, 230.

9. Ibid., p. 196 ref. Li chi 1X.

10. Schoeps, op. cit., p. 198.

11. Ibid.

12. Ibid.

13. Ibid., p. 199.

14. Ibid., p. 197 ref. Li chi, XV.

15. "Analects", XV, p. 23.

16. Schoeps, op. cit., p. 201; also cf. Hutchison, op. cit., p. 199.

17. Ibid.

18. Confucius, Lun Yu, quoted in Schoeps. op. cit., 201.

19. Hutchison, op. cit., p. 199.

20. "Analects", op. cit., V1, 20.

21. Ibid., 111, 17, quoted in Hutchison, op. cit., p. 199.

22. Lin Yutang, The Wisdom of Confucius, Modern Library, New York, 1938, p. 14.

23. Hutchison, op. cit., p. 199.

24. Ibid.

25. Schoeps, op. cit., p. 201, ref. Lun Yu.

26. Hutchison, op. cit., p. 224.

27. Ibid.

28. Fung, op. cit., p. 283.

29. Lin Mousheng, Men and Ideas, John Day, New York, 1943, p. 9.

30. Schoeps, op. cit., p. 205.

31. Wing-Tsit Chan (trans), A Source Book in Chinese Philosophy, Princeton, N. J., 1963, p. 146.

32. Ibid., p. 142.

33. Schpoeps, op. cit., p. 205.

34. Ibid., p. 206.

35. Chan, op. cit., p. 140..

36. Hutchison, op. cit., p. 203.

37. Chan, op. cit., pp. 168, 175; Hutchison, op. cit., pp. 203-8.

38. Schoeps, op. cit., p. 206..

39. Ibid., p. 207.

40. Ibid.

41. Ibid., p. 208.

42. Confucius, quoted in Schoeps, op. cit., p. 209.

43. Schoeps, op.cit., p. 209.

44. Hutchison, op. cit., p. 236.

45. Nakamura, H. The ways of Thinking of Eastern Peoples, Compiled by Japanese National Commission for UNESCO. Tokyo, 1960, p. 527.

46. Ibid., p. 438.

47. Ibid., p. 527.

48. Schoeps, op. cit., p. 211.

49. Ibid.

50. Ibid., p. 213; also cf. Sokyo Ono, Shinto: The Kami Way, Tuttle, Rutland, VT. , 1963, ref. in Hutchison,, op. cit., pp. 237f.

51. Hutchison, op. cit., p. 239.

52. Ibid.; also cf. Schoeps, op. cit., pp. 215f.

53. Schoeps, op. cit., p. 213.

54. Hutchison, op. cit., p. 242.

55. Ibid.

56. Ibid.

57. Schoeps, op. cit., p. 214.

58. Hutchison, op. cit., p. 242.

59. Schoeps. op. cit., p. 215.

60. Ibid.

61. Ibid., p. 217.

62. Ibid., p. 218.

CH. 3: SEMETIC RELIGION: MONOTHEISTIC JUDAISM

The term "Semitic" is derived from the name of one of the sons of Noah, Shem. It is reported that the Prophet Noah, having left Egypt by a boat, landed on the Mount Ararat in Central Asia. Then he asked one of his sons, Shem, to stay in that area (modern Middle-East) and populate it—that is what he did. However, while writing the history of the Middle-East, European historians changed the name from Shem (Shemitic to Semitic).Therefore, the Middle-eastern people are the Semitic people and their religion is named Semitic Religion(s)--- Judaism, Christianity and Islam.

The term monotheism is used for variable usage. However, by and large, it is used for a faith in which one deity is finally fixed. In this book the term is applied to the three Semitic religions, mentioned above. It is also reported that "in its most ancient period Israel's faith was not monotheistic, since the people of Israel acknowledged the existence of other deities, though they sought to serve only One God, Jahweh.... Israel did not achieve monotheism until the time of the prophet Deutero-Isaiah"(1).

The biblical story of Israel's escape from Egyptian bondage in the Book of Exodus is told as the rivalry of two kings—Israel's Lord against the Pharaoh, The god-king of Egypt, ending victorious as the Lord wished and the drowning of his enemy, the pharaoh, and his army.

The Hebrew epic of the Lord and His people must also be seen against the Canaanite or Syrian background of the Ugaritic epic of Baal and Anath, recently found at Ras Shamra(2). While the Lord of Israel has some similarity to the divine heroes of this epic, the differences are more important. It should also be pointed out that Israel's Lord has no divine friends or enemies but lives alone in glory. Baal, Anath, and their children are also deities of nature and culture, whereas Israel's God is believed as Lord of history—at first Israel's history, then mankind's history.

After the above preliminary statements, let us turn to the first Semitic religion—Judaism. The simple definition of the name "Judaism" is the religion of the Jews. Its rise in history has a long history. It is named after one of the twelve Israeli tribes, namely, Judah. We are told that even the pagan Balaam in the biblical tale was compelled to recognise something different in Israel: "Lo, a people dwelling alone, and not reckoning itself among the nations"(Numbers 23: 9).

This especial community came into being by an act of foundation: the tribe of Israel was chosen by God out of the many peoples and led to Sinai, there, as the history is, to be considered worthy of partnership in a divine covenant and to receive the Torah—the commands of the Lord.

Because Israel is believed to be the actual descendent of Father Abraham, the people remained throughout history bound to a common goal: "Their historical task is to testify to the nation's God's supreme rule. The most impressive testimony of this is Israel's mere existence, for it is the only still-living people of antiquity. To that extent, every Jew today by his sheer physical existence is a miracle of divine providence ...." (3).

Among the great religions of the world, Judaism, in respect of the number of followers, is one of the smallest today, but the oldest living religious community. It came to existence out of an alliance of Israeli tribes of Canaan, later called Palestine (approximately from 1550 B.C.). The name Israel,(Genesis 32: 28,) is interpreted to mean "He who strives with God".

One of the interesting stories of the Twelve Tribes of Israel is the story of their "exodus" from Egypt, the long wandering in the desert of Mount Sinai, and the eventual revelation of God's message (Torah) that was granted to them under the leadership of Moses, who became their prophet and thus the transmitter of the divine message. This revelation affected a sacred bond between Yahwe and the tribes of Israel. The tribes acknowledged the God of their forefathers (Israelites) as the ruler of the worlds and Creator of heaven and earth, and Yahwe recognised the Israelites as His followers among the peoples of the world. "The choosing of Israel to be the people of the covenant was accompanied by the establishment of a code of laws consisting of 613 commandments and prohibitions. These are set forth in the Torah (otherwise called the Five Books of Moses, or in Greek, the Pentateuch"(4).

The "Ark of the Covenant" which was with the Israeli settlers, was transferred to Jerusalem by King David (1000—960 B.C.) after he conquered it and made it his capital; later his son, Solomon built a brilliant temple as the main "sanctuary of Israel".

Following the above-mentioned events, focusing around Jerusalem, the kingdom of the Israelites went through a long period of instability with wars between the two main kingdoms of Judah and the kingdom of Israel beginning in 922 and ending in 450 B.C. Since the end of the factional wars in the year, mentioned above, Judaism has represented a careful and conscious amalgamation of religious and national elements. Thus from a common descent of Abraham, there came into being a national religion which in the form given it "by the prophets embodied a universal message, directed toward the whole world"(5).

<u>Unique Themes In Biblical Religion</u>

Considering the Bible against an environment in which nature and society are principal components of the timeless universe, we see first time the unparalleled Hebrew story of the One God who called the Israelites to His service and whose call and service defined and determined Israel's historical existence and historic destiny. Around this main idea of biblical religion, may be bound together a few observable features which placed ancient Israel separate from its environment. There are four such differences: (1) God is Creator; (2) Revelation (3) Human beings as agents (4) History of Drama(6).

<u>Post-Exilic Judaism</u>

The great divide of Old Testament history was the Babylonian exile which extended from 586 B.C. to the capture of Babylon by Cyrus in 539 B.C. In 538 B. C. a small party of the Babylonian Jews set out with the permission of Cyrus to rebuild and repopulate Jerusalem and Judah.

The religious structures which came out in the post-exilic period contained both similarities to and differences from the preexilic tradition of Moses and the prophets. For example, the same conception of God as Lord and Creator—the God of Abraham, of Moses, and of the prophets—continued to be Israel's Lord. But there were important differences: for instance, recovering from the "critical attacks" of the prophets of the eighth and seventh centuries, ritual religion reasserted itself once more. "The temple with its priests and sacrifices stood at the center of society. Such features of Judaism as Torah, Sabbath, the rabbinate, and synagogue, which had been foreshadowed in the writings of Ezekiel, began to assume their historic shape during the postexilic period"(7).

After a long period of political turmoil—from the end of the exilic period to the end of the biblical period--Judah was a subordinate province of both Persian and Greek empires, and then later after a century of independence under the Maccabees

(164-63 B.C.), of the Roman Empire, Israel's religious life became the important point of its existence. As a result, "Four main patterns of religion assumed definite form during this time: (1) priestly and legal Judaism, (2) devotional Judaism, (3) wisdom literature and piety, and (4) apocalypse (8).

The Jewish Creed

It is important to state clearly that Judaism has certain specific doctrines: it teaches the unity and oneness of God (Yahweh), who revealed His will, the Torah to the Jews at Sinai headed by Moses. This revelation was continued first in the prophets (Isaiah, Jeremiah, Ezekiel, Amos, Hosea, etc). In addition, the Jews believe that the world is God's creation—dates 5726 years ago (9). Worship of God as the Ruler of the universe is one of the fundamental acts. Thus the Jewish creed says: "Hear O Israel: The Lord our God is one Lord"(Deuteronomy 6: 4). Thus the intercessor figure or Son of God theory is rejected. Similarly, the theory of original sin is rejected because it is viewed as an unavoidable compulsion to sin, but an inborn or inherent inclination in man toward evil is recognised. Judaism believes in the resurrection of the dead and reward and punishment according to man's good and evil deeds: "It expects the coming of the Messiah or of the messianic age in which the evil impulses will be extirpated from men's hearts and an eternal kingdom of peace will 'dawn'. For this reason, Judaism rejects the Christian belief that salvation has already taken place, or at least has begun"(10).The famous Jewish religious philosopher, Maimonides (1135—1204), in his commentary on the Mishna summerised the content of the Jewish creed in thirteen doctrinal truths(11).

At this stage it should be pointed out that the origins of prophecy in the Bible go far back in history. Later ages looked back to Moses as the model or archetypal prophet, and the idea of ethical religion is traceable to him. Later, during Israel's first centuries in Palestine, a group of Yahweh enthusiasts wandered the countryside prophesying, singing, dancing, working themselves into ecstatic states. Saul is reported to have identified himself with one such band.

Biblical prophecy began to take on a new measurement or dimension of ethical and social criticism in such figures as Nathan in David's time and Ahija in Solomon's. Unlike other religions, in ancient Israel this kind of religious criticism was considered important. Prophecy assumed a new significance in the "great Elijah" of the ninth century. He was defender of both social justice and national independence.

<u>Jewish Ritual and Worship</u>

For many reasons, Judaism is popularly known as a "family religion". For an orthodox family, the whole life is guided or conditioned by religious matters. "Affix to the door to the home is a mezuzah, a small capsule containing fifteen verses from scripture, signifying that the house serves God just as does the synagogue as a place of assembly for the faithful, a temple of God. The dietary laws of the Torah, which again are religious in nature, being means for the sanctification of Israel, are faithfully observed."(12).

It should be stated clearly that the flesh of impure animals such as the swine is forbidden.

This prohibition is more demonological than hygienic, "for the pig was a sacred animal in the cult of the god Moloch" (13). Furthermore, the law also prohibits the consumption of snake, regarded as demonic, carrion, mammals and birds that are not slaughtered in prescribe way, also certain parts of the fat and blood, which according to ancient oriental ideas was the seat of the soul. The proper way or method of slaughtering by the kosher butcher aims at complete bleeding of the meat that is intended for human consumption. Equally, under ban are animals which prove to have diseased internal organs. There is also a particular prohibition against eating the muscles of the hip in animals, for in Jacob's night struggle the angel dislocated his hip. "Therefore, to this day the Israelites do not eat the sinew of the hip which is upon the hollow of the thigh, because he touched the hollow of Jacob's thigh on the sinew of the hip"(Genesis, 32:32).

Another important requirement of Judaism is the prayer at home or in the synagogue. That means, in Judaism the domestic home is as important as the community-based synagogue for religious purposes. And the fundamental form of such prayer is the <u>beracha</u> (prayer of praise and thanksgiving, hymn), which must be done with intensity or seriousness (14).

It should be mentioned here that in Judaism worship is the same all through the year; the main prayer texts have remained the same since the beginning of this religion, and are the same for all Jews all over the world. For instance, on festival days, additional texts are used. Also, certain symbolic acts of temple worship in Jerusalem, such as the blowing of the shofar, have also been continued in modern time services.

Regular reading of the scriptures is an essential part of the Jewish religious practices. One section is read on every <u>Sabbath</u> (Saturday).There are also readings required from the prophetic books. It should also be stated here that one of the very important requirements of Jewish religious and family life is the Sabbath. Rabbis frequently praised the "Sabbath as a foretaste of the world to come. On this day orthodox Jews refrain from all works, do not travel, use the telephone, write or touch money"(15). These traditional Sabbath restrictions have given the orthodox Jews the seventh day as a day of rest—one of Jewish most "important institutions". To add to what is stated above is the fact that the synagogue Sabbath worship starts at sunset on Friday evening, and continues up to the home evening meal, "at which time the housewife lights the traditional Sabbath candles and the father of the family blesses the wine and breaks the Sabbath bread"(16).

Regarding the religious holidays of the Jewish tradition, we are told that main holidays of the Jewish year are the "New Year" (in September or October), "and Yom Kippur, the Day of Atonement" to drive a goat into the desert "who shall bear all the iniquities of the children of Israel, and all their transgressions, all their sins" (Leviticus 16: 21-22). By the way, it is well-known that from that custom follows the idea of the "scape-goat". This is a time of ten-day period of penitence, recollection and return to God.

There are a few important holidays of the "liturgical year is the Feast of Passover" (in March or April), remembering the time when the "Angel of Death passed over the houses of the Israelites in Egypt" (Exod. 12). "The prayers and dietary prescripts of the passover meal (seder) are set forth in detail in the Haggadah. The thin, unleavened breads are the 'bread of affliction' " (Deutero-Isaiah16: 3). It should be mentioned here that at that meal time, "the father of the family, holding a piece of matzoth in his raised hand speaks the traditional words: 'This is the bread of affliction that our fathers ate in Egypt; whoever is hungry let him come and eat with us"(17).

Finally, let us say a few words about the pilgrimage feasts: Shavuot, the Feast of Weeks or First Fruits (in May or June), which is meant to be as a reminder of the reception of the Ten Commandments; "Sukkoth, the Feast of Tabernacles, an eight-day harvest thanksgiving in the fall; the Feast of Lights, Chanukah,...celebrates the victory of Judas Maccabaeus over the Syrians and the re- lighting of the temple light. Each evening of the eight-day festival one more candle is lit in the eight-armed candelabrum, and children receive presents. Chanukah, like Purim in the spring--which is a kind of Jewish carnival--is a festival of joy recalling the rescue of the Jews from oppression"(18).

Apart from the feast days, mentioned above, Jewish ceremonial also follows the course of human life. "On the eighth day, after birth, boys are circumcised (Gen. 17.10) "as a sign of the covenant between God and Israel and in memory of God's covenant with Abraham. At the age of thirteen boys become a bar mitzvah, a son of the law" and starts the religious duties like an adult. The other important events in life, such as "marriage and death, are subordinated to man's duties toward" Yahweh and have their particular ceremonial expressions (19).

In Judaism there is no priesthood and no priestly institution as in Christianity. The synagogue is for worship. Every individual Jew is responsible for his/her religious obligations. The rabbi is only a prayer-leader, religious teacher and judge in matters of religious rule or law. There are several voluntary Jewish association which deal only with administrative questions. These organisations not only deal with communities' purely religious matters but also deal with dietary laws by appointing kosher butchers. Usually, the congregation is also supposed to have a bathhouse, which menstruating women are supposed to use according to the conditions laid down in the Bible. Another important character or feature of the orthodox Jewish congregation is the "Holy Brotherhood", which takes the responsibilities of "washing, anointing and burying the dead without distinction of position and economic condition of the members of the community. Service in this brotherhood is performed on an honorary basis"(20).

Ethics In Judaism

In Judaism, righteousness is the top-ranking ethical quality. From this rule of ethics, it follows that man has ethical responsibilities both toward God and all man. These responsibilities are set in the laws of Moses, in the proclamations of the prophets and in later interpretations. That is to say, in Judaism ethics is an integral part of religion. "The Hebrew idea of Kadosh (holy) as the supreme standard of existence and conduct merges ethics and religion: 'you shall be holy, for I the Lord your God am holy'"(Leviticus 19: 2). In Judaism, the highest quality of God is righteousness; and "since man was created in the image of God", it is his top obligation to live in accord with God's qualities that He taught Moses on Mount Sinai: "The Lord, the Lord, a God merciful and gracious, slow to anger, and abounding in steadfast love and faithfulness, keeping steadfast love for thousands, forgiving iniquity and transgression and sin"(Exd. 34:6-7). Likewise, in Deuteronomy 13: 4 the command is given: "You shall walk after the Lord your God". The Talmud offers the following interpretation for the above command: "Is it possible for men to walk after the deity, when it is said after all: "The Lord your God is a devouring fire"? In fact, man must follow the ways in which God works: the way he visits the sick (Abraham in the Grove of Mamre); the way he consoles the mourner (Isaac after Abraham's death); the way he buries the dead (burial of Moses)-- so shall man act. God defined what was good for man in the Torah; ethics develops out of the commandment to love your neighbor as yourself"(Leviticus,19: 18).

Interestingly, no ethical distinction is drawn between Jews and non-Jews. This is clear from the laws about non-Jews in the Bible: "When a stranger sojourns with you in your land, you shall not do him wrong. The stranger who sojourns with you shall be to you as the native among you, and you shall love him as your self; for you were strangers in the land of Egypt, I am the Lord your God (Leviticus. 19: 33-34). "Robbery, blackmail, theft, embezzlement, any appropriation of the property of others, are considered a sin against God as well as offence against man. All trickery in trading is forbidden; any business dealings that violate good morals are invalid before the law; excessive profits, price-gouging and unfair competition are decried. For 'let the property of your neighbor be as dear to you as your own'" (from the Talmud tract Proverbs of the Fathers 2: 12).In post-biblical times charitable institutions were established to suite changed social situation. "Those who refused were likened by the Talmud to idolaters. Jewish charitable activities have persisted through the centuries; originally only individual and plan-less, they developed in the nineteenth and twentieth centuries into great international associations of Jewish welfare and social organizations, ..."(21).

The Talmud

It is a well-known fact that man's ethical duties toward God and toward his fellow-human-beings are set forth in the

Bible (Torah). But how these rules were to be related to the daily life of later Jews who lived later in a totally different situation was the content of the Talmud (Mishna and Gemara). Even in biblical age many instructions relation to the fulfilling of the rules of the Torah had been handed down by oral traditions. These were collected and written down in the Mishna (completed around 200 C.E. by Rabbi Yehuda ha-nassi(22).

The huge material of the Talmud are divided into Halakah and Haggada. The former is the part of the Talmud that deals with the 613 rules of the Torah (according to rabbinical count: 248 commandments and 365 prohibitions) in their specific applications. The latter, on the other hand, contains more narrative material; ethical teachings, proverbial wisdom, legends, parables, sermons and allegorical tales. However, only the Halakah has the obligatory force of religious law. The latter, on the other hand, is more concerned with stimulating or rousing the emotions. It should be mentioned here that "Both Halakah and Haggada were elaborated and exposited in the frequently poetical or allegorical Midrash, which attempted to draw lessons for the present from the past"(23).

The special character and spirit of the Haggadah can be seen from a few "edifying fragments taken from the <u>Proverbs of</u>

the Fathers, a Mishna tract which contains no Halakhic doctrines, but only proverbial wisdom of a religious nature"(24)

Development of Jewish Mysticism

Along with the Talmudic line of doctrine, there has appeared since early times a mystical element in Judaism, which developed strong during the Middle Ages. The Jewish mysticism reflected an "existential" experience in which the subject-object dichotomy of intellectual cognition are left behind. This mysticism is hard to understand because there is a closed cosmological system underlying it, and it has gone through many stages of development. Speculations on the "hoped-for", soon coming of the Messiah are tightly linked with almost all clearly revealed characters of Jewish mysticism.

This mysticism spread from Spain and Southern France in the thirteenth century C.E. It is a well-known fact that this mysticism was the result of Muslim Mysticism (Sufism) in the Iberian Peninsula. "It incorporated, under the name of Cabbala, older traditions, some of which probably stemmed from ancient Gnosticism. Its principal document, the Book of Sohar ('radiance'), written in... Aramaic, was ascribed to Rabbi Simon bar Yochai and supposedly dated from the second century"(25). However, some suggest that the commentary on the Pentateuch was probably written by Moshe ben Shemtob de Leon of Guadalahara, (a cabbalist who died in 1305). The Book of Sohar was first published in Cremona and Mantua in 1558.

The main themes of the Jewish mysticism are the following: "The major themes of Jewish mysticism are the state of being before the creation, and the primordial light above the visible sky; the doctrine of the ten spheres, which are permeated by divinity; the conception that heavenly sparks in all earthly things must be liberated from their husks. In addition, there are allegorical interpretation of the deeper meanings of the Torah, based on numerological manipulation of the Hebrew letters; similar interpretations of biblical persons and of all of Jewish history; and an extensive doctrine dealing with angels and demons"(26). Since there are such evil powers from the "other side" in the world we live, "practical Cabbala" also deals "in magic and counter-spells". The ultimate goal of Cabbalistic efforts, however, is "spiritual understanding of the ultimate mysteries and hence the *unio mystica* of man, made in God's image, with the *deus absconditus*, the hidden God"(27).

Recent Development in Judaism

Throughout the Middle Ages the forms of Judaism remained more or less unchanged. Unlike the previous time, when the Jews had been in ghettos isolated from their surroundings, the opening of the ghettos resulted in a revolutionary upheaval for European Jews. Within a generation or so, they had to comprehend an intellectual evolution. The reformers tried to eliminate ghetto mentality in order to make the Jews capable of taking their place in society with all their rights and obligation like other citizens of the society at large. As a result, "during the century of emancipation the traditional forms of worship were increasingly abandoned or transformed. However, the religious liberals did not succeed in establishing a generally binding new way of life which would bring the religious laws of biblical and post-biblical times into conformity with the realities of the nineteenth and twentieth centuries"(28).

The time of liberation, begun by the work of Moses Mendelssohn (1729-1786) and the effects of the French Revolution, adversely affected the traditional forms of Judaism. Since then, Judaism has been split into three schools, namely, orthodox, conservative and liberal, resulting from different approaches to issues of religious practice, rather than to basic issues of religious belief (only extreme liberals and Zionists have demanded a revision of their religion to bring it closer to the views and practices of non-believers or believers in other religions). The establishment of the state of Israel in 1948, with its official language of Hebrew--a modernized Biblical Hebrew

(Ivrith)-- begun a new phase in the history of the people and religion of Israel. In the state of Israel only about twenty percent of all can be identified as orthodox. A large number of Jews regard their world-wide spread as their mission and therefore reject nationalistic boundaries.

CH. 3 : FOOTNOTES

SEMITIC RELIGION--MONOTHEISTIC JUDAIM

1. Hutchison, John A., <u>Paths of Faith</u>, Mcgrow Hill Book Company, Montreal, 1969, p. 291, also cf. Smith, W. Roberson, <u>The Religion of the Semites</u>: <u>The Fundamental Institutions</u>, Schocken Books, New York, 1972.

2. Mendelson, I., <u>Religions of the Ancient Near East</u>, Liberal Arts, New York, 1955, pp. 223f.

3. Schoeps, Hans-Joachim, <u>The Religions of Mankind</u>: <u>Their Origin and Development</u> (translated from the German by Richard and Clara Winston), A Doubleday Anchor Book, Garden City, New York, 1968, p. 221.

4. <u>Ibid</u>.

5. <u>Ibid.</u>, p. 222.

6. Hutchison, <u>op. cit.</u>, p.292.

7. <u>Ibid.</u>, p. 318.

8. <u>Ibid</u>.

9. Schoeps, <u>op. cit.</u>, p. 222.

10. <u>Ibid.</u>, p. 223.

11. Cf. <u>Ibid.</u>, pp. 223f..

12. <u>Ibid.</u>, p. 224.

13. Ibid.

14. Ibid., p. 225.

15. Ibid., p. 226.

16. Ibid.

17. Ibid., p. 227.

18. Ibid.

19. Ibid., p. 228.

20. Ibid.

21. Ibid., p. 230.

22. Ibid.

23. Ibid., p. 231.

24. Ibid.

25. Ibid., p. 232.

26. Ibid., p. 233.

27. Ibid.

28. Ibid., p. 236.

Ch. 4: Jesus And Christian Origins

It should be stated at the outset that "Christianity began as a movement within first-century Judaism; its founder lived and died a devout, though heretical and schismatic, Jew"(1) What is more important, Christianity has always firmly maintained its Hebraic heritage against those who would deny or distort that heritage in theory or in practice. Nonetheless, by the beginning of the second century, Christianity was a Gentile religious movement of the Greco-Roman world, speaking in the Greek language and thought forms and living in a society whose political institutions and leadership were Roman. However, within four hundred years, in the brisk competition of faiths in that world,

Christianity came out on top, becoming the official religion of Constantine's empire.

It is also stated that "The Jewish heritage of Christianity began with the full acceptance of the Jewish Bible as holy scripture, which included the authority of the biblical images and ideas of God and human beings, of good and evil, or human origin and destiny. It meant that Christianity was a species of biblical monotheism—the second of the three monotheistic faiths, to assume its distinctive historical shapes and forms."(2).

Life of Jesus

Apart from a few oral fragments in classical and Jewish literature, the fundamental source of knowledge of life and teachings of Jesus is the New Testament, and more particularly the Four Gospels. "The first three Gospels—Mathew, Mark and Luke—taken together, show a common outline for the life and teachings of Jesus, in contrast to the Gospel of John", which differs sharply in order and point of view of the first three (called Synoptic Gospels since they "view together" the life and teachings of Jesus) but the questions arose: "who wrote them, when, where, and under what circumstances?"(3)

The answer appears to be that soon following the "life" of Jesus there was a time of oral tradition. Perhaps the first written source was an assumptive or hypothetical document to which modern scholars have given the name Q ("source"). According to scholarly assumption or understanding, Q consisted primarily of selections of Jesus' teachings, perhaps "topically arranged and used for instructional purposes within the Christian community". Some of these documents were possibly "in existence by ten or twenty years after Jesus' 'death'" that is, by C.E. 40 or 50.

It is well-known that more than four accounts of Jesus' life gained circulation or publicity in the early Christian operation. Of these, the three Synoptics finally won popularity, gaining prominence in the New Testament.

Teaching In Galilee

According to Mark's Gospel, Jesus first appeared openly in Galilee, saying "The time is fulfilled, and the kingdom of God is at hand".(4). The theme of his preaching was the imminent coming of the Kingdom of God and the conditions for citizenship in the Kingdom. Apart from preaching, "he is reported to have healed the sick, to have performed exorcisms and to have done many other "mighty works". On that occasion, he gathered to himself twelve intimate disciples. Having instructed them, he sent them out to spread his message throughout Galilee. From the beginning of his public preaching, there were loud voices of hostility from Jewish leaders.

For how long Jesus preached at Galilee is unknown. Opinions vary from six months to two years. If he was successful there, why did he not leave that place for other places like Tyre, Sidon, Caesarea and Philippi?(5).

Confession of Messiahship

All the Synoptic Gospels record the scene as they walked along the road near Caesarea Phillipi; Jesus asked disciples: "Who do men say that I the Son of Man am?"(6).The reply was that some thought he was Elijah, (there was a popular legend that Elijah would return just before the Messiah). Others thought he was John the Baptist—come back to life after his murder. "But who do you say that I am?" persisted Jesus. To this, Peter, speaking for himself and the others, responded, "You are the Christ the Son of the living God".

This discourse must be taken against the background of first-century Judaism's exciting messianic expectation. According to the Synoptics, this was the first occasion Jesus spoke openly and directly of the messiahship. He spoke, though only privately, within the circle of his followers, "elliptically", evoking Peter's confession rather than making a definite assertion. "Later at the end of his life, standing before the Sanhedrin, Jesus was to make his first public statement on this issue in reply to the high priest's question"(7).

It should be stated that "The question of Jesus' messianic claim is of crucial significance to Christianity, for Christianity is by definition the religion of those who believe Jesus to be the Christ. Later, other terms came to be used as synonyms for this original title, such as Lord, Saviour, Word and Son of God; but they were attempts to find adequate Gentile, Greek synonyms for the original Hebrew title of messiah. Christianity began with the apostolic confession of Jesus as the Christ, or Messiah."(8)

Teachings of Jesus

We are told that Jesus' primary teaching was the Kingdom of God or Kingdom of Heaven. In first century Judaism, this term referred to the historic age of fulfillment which was believed to be at hand, the messianic age to which all Israel looked forward anxiously. Jesus' Kingdom of God is his way of saying the same thing.

The idea of a reign of God over the entire world had been a part of biblical religion from the beginning of the Old Testament days. But according to Israeli prophets, God's rule was not now at hand, rather human-kings seemed to be effectively in charge of the world's destiny. Therefore, "the prophets appealed to a future age when God's whole will would be done over all the world. Such was the origin of the Kingdom of God" (9).

Jesus' view appears to be completely different from his contemporaries' view about the features of Kingdom. In his view, it is reported "each individual by humble repentance made his or her way into the kingdom, whose membership included people of every race and nation. The requirements of citizenship as Jesus set them forth in the sermon on the mount were fundamentally moral in nature"(10).

Commenting on the Jesus' idea of the "kingdom of God", one writer says: "While Jesus' kingdom of God was essentially a universal human brotherhood", there is no foundation in his teachings for recognising the kingdom with any special kind of society or social organisation. Obviously, "When Jesus spoke of the Kingdom of God, he was not envisaging democracy, socialism, or any other ism. Rather he was dealing with a radically different sort of problem, namely, the state of the human world in which God's whole will would be done."(11)

It goes without saying that there is no reason for separation of religion from ethics in Jesus' teaching; rather they are two aspects of a single reality, religion being the mental allegiance of the human heart, and morality, the conduct which sprang from this source.

The main religious reality in Jesus' teaching was God, "conceived as lord and creator of all that exists, and as supreme object of human devotion". In his teaching, Jesus' main argument was not God's existence, rather was the relation of humans to God. Thus, it was his view that the main reason for the existence of mankind—"its purpose on earth"—"is to do the will of God" or service to Him by all means.

According to Jesus, the content of the divine will for human life can be summed up in the single word—love. "Jesus used this word to mean a spontaneous, whole hearted, and complete affirmation of the selfhood of other."(12). Contrary to much of the present-day opinion, this teaching is not unprecedented by any means: this is a well-known teaching in all religions with an ultimate reality especially in all Semitic religions. However, it must be emphasised that in Jesus' mind, the concept of love had a strict meaning which is absent in modern sentimental usage. "To him, love included justice and judgment as well as mercy.... It is accurate to summarize Jesus' God as sovereign love. It is a sovereignty which is now hidden, but which will be manifested fully in the coming of the Kingdom."(13).

The main moral commandments of Jesus had an unconditional feature based on a divine "Thou shalt...," and the commandments were all summed up in the single supreme commandment: "Thou shalt love thy neighbor as thyself."(14)

The main theme of Jesus' faith and ethic is expressed in his own summary of the Torah and the Prophets: "You shall love the Lord your God with all your heart, and with all your soul and mind and strength, and your neighbor as yourself."(Mark 12: 28-31). This famous statement is a double quotation by Jesus of (1) Deuteronomy 6: 4—5 and (2) Leviticus 19: 18. "The basic moral virtue is love conceived as respect for, and affirmation of, personality as made in the divine image (15).

To Jesus, neighbour-love was something more inward than any precious legal code. "It was an attitude of the heart; and from the heart, Jesus reminded his hearers, I proceed the attitudes that govern actions"(Mathew 5:17f). It should be emphasised that it was such an attitude whose "universality" extended beyond all obstacles of race and colour or class to the limits of humanity. It was exactly "this universality which was the subject of such teachings as the parable of the good Samaritan(16).

Commenting on the above, Hutchison draws our attention to the following: "In contrast to the good as love, evil for Jesus was an ever-present self-centeredness which sets humans against God and their neighbors. Sometimes it is manifested as trust in one's possessions as with the Rich Fool, sometimes as the pride of the Pharisees who 'trusted in themselves and despised the others' "(17).

Finally, the important issue was the relation or connection of Jesus' faith and ethic to Judaism and to the whole Hebraic heritage of the Old Testament: "For one thing, Jesus' teachings were inward and more internationalist or universal than most first-century interpretations of the Torah. He stood against code morality and against the prevalent nationalism of his time. Yet in both respects, Jesus stood squarely on the classical tradition of Torah and the Prophets. Indeed Jesus seems to have regarded his teaching as the fulfillment of the Torah and the Prophets"(18).

THE NEW TESTAMENT CHRISTIAN COMMUNITY

The Resurrection of Christ

Christ's resurrection was the crucial fact for the beginning of the New Testament Christian Community. At the crucifixion, Jesus' followers fled and left for their native Galilee. However, after a few weeks they returned to Jerusalem with a changed attitude. "They were the servants of a living faith which within a century was to make its impact felt from one end of the Roman empire to the other, and which in the next four centuries would turn that empire upside down."(19).

What is the cause for revolutionary change? One writer attempts to answer the question: The traditional answer is the resurrection of Christ—"an event which convinced the followers of Jesus that he was not dead but alive—more living and more powerful than in the days of his flesh. Hence, the resurrection might be defined as that event which certified to the Christian community the living spirit of Christ as an ever-present reality."(20).

Dealing with the crucial question of Christ's "resurrection", there are many opinions even though none of them is rational. Let us quote the opinion of the apostle Paul wrote to the Corinthian Church:

"For I delivered to you as of first importance what I also received, that Christ died for our sins in accordance with the scriptures, that he was buried, that he was raised on the third day in accordance with the scriptures, and that he appeared to Cephas, then to the twelve. Then he appeared to more than five hundred brethren at one time, most of whom are still alive, though some have fallen asleep.

Then he appeared to James, then to all the apostles. Last of all, as to one untimely born, he appeared also to me"(21).

The Early Jerusalem Community

It is well-known that the Pentecost marked the starting event of the Christian movement and community, which made of, at the beginning, of a few small groups of Jesus' followers who spread religious propaganda in Jerusalem. It is also reported that an event of top-ranking significance to this group occurred "on the Jewish Feast of Pentecost in the same year that Jesus 'died'" (31-33 C. E.). In this regard, Peter addressed the multitude and according to the information available in the Book of Acts, 3,000 converts were made to the new religion. (22). (Pentecost was the festival which "commemorated" the giving of the Torah on the Mount Sinai; "and according to rabbinic tradition it had been given in the seventy languages of humankind"). It is stated that the Christian story was a kind of "deliberate parallel" describing the giving of the New Testament in different languages.

According to another version of the same story, we are told that Jesus did not want to establish the Christian Church or Community, but it proceeded directly from his life and ministry when he called his followers to the approaching Kingdom of God. "The original hearers of these tidings formed the nucleus of the first Christian community"(23). The history of early Christianity exemplifies the way a new messianic movement started out of belief in the "resurrection of Jesus". According to the account in Acts 3:18 f., the first Christian community of Jerusalem began with the "descent of the Holy Spirit on the first Pentecost, and was expressed by an actual speaking of foreign tongues". That was an indication to the community that they themselves belonged to the Last Days, "for Jewish eschatology predicted this outpouring of the spirit in those days"(24).

To end the present discussion, let us say: "To their contemporaries, they must have appeared as one more harebrained sect. What made them appear even more eccentric was their firm conviction that Jesus had been raised from the dead, that he was spiritually present in the community of believers, and that he would soon return to earth in power to rule over God's Kingdom"(Acts 1: 4).

<u>Pauline Theology</u>

We are told that more than any other person, Paul was the father of Christian theology. His thinking was the present of his mind to the events in which he played an important role. As is well known, Pal was a Jew who found the Messiah in Jesus. The phrase like "Jesus is Christ", and "Jesus is Lord" run like a chorus through Paul's writings. Without any doubt, his thought manifested an important influence from Greek mystery religions and philosophy, but the basis of it remained fundamentally "Hebraic". For instance, his God was the God of his Jewish fathers, namely, "the sovereign Lord who created and ruled the universe", who had spoken to human beings through His Prophets like Moses and other prophets, and who had now spoken again a final word to Jesus Christ, as Paul believed.

For Paul, Christianity was a new covenant, a new revelation of God to humanity. As the "old covenant" focused on the giving of the Torah to Moses, so the "new covenant" focused on Jesus Christ. Paul called Jesus a <u>Lord</u>. But going beyond this, he came at length to think of Christ as a "preexistent divine figure who had condescended to take on human form, who in his death struggled victoriously with cosmic forces of evil, and who now reigned with God in heavenly places."(25).

The Fourth Gospel

This Gospel is usually attributed to the disciple John, but the recent time biblical study has shown this to be very unlikely. Writing around year 100, perhaps in the city of Ephesus, its author seems to be "familiar with the language and thought of current Greek philosophy and religion"(26).

Jesus was considered as the "incarnate word, or Logos, of God". By the way, Philo Judaeus of Alexandria interpreted the term "Logos as a cosmic intermediary between God and humans, active in all creation." The word Logos was destined to achieve "widespread use in the next century in Gnostic philosophies". It was this popular idea which the "Fourth Gospel appropriated and used for the interpretation of Jesus. It asserted in effect that the basic meaning and structure of the universe was incarnated in Jesus' Life."(27).

Christianity at the Early Stages: Church and Empire

By 100 C.E., Christianity had spread all over the Greco-Roman Empire but at the same time suffered oppression by Nero and Domitian. It is reported that for Romans, "the Christian movement was only one more of the 'oriental superstitions' which had lately spread all over the "empire with bizarre rites and irrational beliefs"(28). The Romans would like to see the end of the matter. But there were malicious propaganda about the Christians. For example, there was rumour that they worshipped a king other than Caesar; also they refused to perform the rituals to Caesar--a sort of rites which most Romans thought "as no more religious than the modern flag salute. Many Christians avoided military and public services. Christians often incurred the charge of atheism for their scornful attitude toward the old gods. There were also ugly rumors of cannibalism in Christian worship"(29).

The disagreement of Christ and Christ and Caesar persisted for more than three centuries but came to an end with Christianity as the official religion of Constantine's empire. However, the conflict continued until at last in 64 C.E. Domitian tried a more organised action all over the empire. Trajan

(98—117) is known for his letter to Pliny the younger, advising what both men must have regarded as a lenient course against the Christian offensive. "Christians were not to be hunted out, and if they were willing to sacrifice, they were to be discharged. Only they persisted in their refusal to perform the prescribed rites were they to be punished.(30).

Beginning of Christian Theologies

As Christianity came increasingly under Roman criticism, explanations were given. They appeared in a type of writing called apologia for Christianity. The newly converted Christians, having no adequate philosophy, yet found Christianity true. Among these Christians were philosophers such as "Quadratus and later Aristides, Melito, Bishop of Sardis, the author of the Epistle to Diognetus and Justin Martyr, who was a teacher of Stoicism, Aristotelianism, Pythagoreanism and Platonism" (Justin's Apology op. cit., p. 8). To Justin, regarding God as neutral between good and evil is immoral. The new life to which humans are called by Christ is a life of love for God and for fellow-human beings. To Justin, Christianity is higher in position for possessing the appearance or body shape, and teachings of Jesus Christ, who over and above had come in fulfillment of Old Testament "prophecy".

It should also be mentioned that Justin made extensive use of the Logos in his interpretation of Christ. To him, the Logos is that aspect of the divine nature by which humans are guided to think rationally and live rationally and righteously. "By this power, Justin argued, both the philosophers of Greece and the prophets of Israel lived and taught; any rational being, even though professing atheism, lives by this power"(31).

Heresy and Orthodoxy

As Christianity began to spread in the Greco-Roman Empire, many kinds of "theological interpretation" developed; some of them were openly inconsistent with each other. Out of this situation developed the idea of unorthodoxy or heresy and its opposite, orthodoxy. These ideas were obviously related to the theological orientation of early Christianity.

"The earliest Christian confessions, dating from New Testament times and used as baptismal formulas, were simple statements such as 'Jesus is Lord'. By the middle of the second century the simple formula had grown to a series of fixed questions and answers, having many of the phrases of the Apostle's Creed, though the final formulation of the Apostle's Creed cannot be traced to a date earlier than the eighth century."(23).

Many of the questions disclosed in the "Apostle's Creed are those of the second-century struggle of Christianity with Gnosticism and,...,with the teachings of Marcion in the Roman church". <u>Gnosticism</u>—is a collection "of philosophic and religious tendencies of the later Greco-Roman world". By and large, "the Gnostics maintained a dualist cosmology in which the world was" considered both good and real, and a domain of matter believed to be evil or unreal or both(24).

<u>Development of Episcopal Authority</u>

The church of New Testament times was very ordinary in both organisation and worship. The apostles or bishops were authorities in worship and administration; in both matters of the church's life, this leadership was wonderfully executed. However, with the passage of time, all this changed. Resident bishops claiming authority by apostolic succession unfairly replaced dynamic leaders, "and worship moved in the direction of formality". "About 50, he[Resident Bishop] was of the church who had received baptism and the Holy Spirit and called Jesus, Lord; about 180 he who acknowledged the rule of faith, the New Testament canon and the authority of bishops"(25).

<u>Worship and Sacraments</u>

"Christian worship and devotional practices, plus church organisation," went through development in the direction of formalism. But an important feature was an increasing routine in the celebration of Eucharist. "From the charismatic, spirit-filled celebration of the of the New Testament times, both practice and theory assumed ever-increasing formalism"(26).The Eucharist could be celebrated only by the duly enacted priests, and the congregation was held after "a period of catechetical instruction" and limited to members of the church. Rapidly people began to believe emphatically that the bread and wine were the body and blood of Christ, which would generate eternal life. "The Eucharist was increasingly regarded as a reenactment of Christ's sacrifice on the cross. It became the central and crucial act of Christian worship"(27).

It should be mentioned that the Eucharist worship was usually held on Sunday, but also on other days. However, the great "event" of the year was "Easter, celebrating Christ's resurrection". It should also be mentioned that the forty days of "Lent leading up to Easter", and even more days of the week preceding, "commemorated Christ's suffering and death". By the way, Easter is also a period of happiness or rejoicing; prayers for the dead and respect "of martyrs were an increasingly important theme of Christian worship"(28). It should be mentioned here that in importance, the sacrament of baptism is second to the Eucharist.

Eastern Orthodox Christianity

Since the beginning of Christianity, there was a visible division between the East and the West. The division was from Europe all the way to the Adriatic Sea to the continent of Africa; to the west in Spain, Gaul and Italy up to Rome; east of it is the Balkan Peninsula, Asia Minor and the Near East up to Constantinople. We are told that the Christianity of the West tended to be active, pragmatic, and legal, while that of the East tended to be contemplative, mystical and passive. As centuries passed, the two drifted further apart. Their differences widened and deepened until two forms of Christianity emerged as historic facts.

From the beginning, some eastern bishops opposed the claims to first in rank of the bishop of Rome. In the east, the pope's declarations were sometimes officially ignored and sometimes rejected. Eventually, the pope's claims, central to Roman Catholicism, appeared in the East but were regarded as "schismatic". These trends were strengthened by events of non-religious history. As the western empire declined, the papacy was thrown into the "vacuum of power"; holding both political and religious leadership for the people of Rome and Italy as a whole. However, in the East there was no such decline, the imperial organisation or structure being renewed and maintained by rulers like Justinian (527—565), and the Byzantine emperors of Constantinople held the church closely, thus creating a dependent relationship of church to state which eventually became the main feature of Eastern Orthodoxy.

We have already seen Christianity newly emerged from the "catacombs" and the established religion of Constantine's empire. During the same period, it was divided into Eastern Orthodoxy and Roman (Western) Catholicism, although the formal break between them did not come until 1054 C.E. over the issue of the rights of Roman Catholic Christians in Constantinople. Now we return to Catholic Christianity as the formative religion of the new civilization (West/Europe).

Augustine's Life and Thought

Nowhere is the historic transition from Greco-Roman antiquity to the new or nascent civilization of the West more clearly visible than in the life and thought of Saint Augustine (354—430 C.E.). His life is recorded in his <u>Confessions</u>, which has the form of a discourse between himself and God. In the presence of his God, Augustine discovered his human self.

Augustine was born in Tagaste, Numidia, North Africa, the son of a devout Christian mother and a pagan father. After his education at Carthage, he began a career of travelling "rhetorist", teaching continuously in Carthage, Rome and Milan. "At the same time, he rejected as childish his mother's Christianity and began a period of spiritual wondering among the faiths and philosophies of the time. His first excursion was into the dualistic system called <u>Manichaeism</u>. Disillusioned by the inability of its leading exponent, Faustus, to answer his questions, Augustine shifted to the skepticism of the New Academy"(29).

The Monastic Orders

In the broadest possible description, the Christian styles of asceticism and monasticism should be realised as distinct diversifications on themes which recur all over the world's religions.

In the Medieval West, monasticism was to become a main institution of society. General people in consecutive generations accepted monastic views of discarding the world. Still, ironically, these monks vigorously helped to build the new culture of Europe, and to maintain and guide its life. Lynn White has tried to interpret Medieval Christianity as a succession of three great waves of reformation.(30).

The Dominican order was founded by Dominic, a Spaniard (1170-1221). who on a visit through southern France was dismayed at the disregard shown to Catholic Christianity by a large heretical movement and schism by the "Albigensian Cathari". Dominic wanted to do something to win these people; as a result, he founded the Order of Preachers, widely known as Dominicans, in 1215 and was given the official approval of the church the following year. The Dominicans followed the Franciscans in adopting the rule of mendicancy. It is also well-known that the new order was organised into provinces with elected officials, thus sharing "authority with representative government"(31).

The new movement spread quickly all over Europe, especially to universities. Some of the well-known persons of this faith were Albert the Great and Thomas Aquinas, who were Scholastic philosophers, Tauler and Eckhart, who were mystics, and Savonarola, the preacher. Eventually, it was the intellectual quality and moral integrity of the Dominicans which led to their selection as inquisitors.

Finally, the monastic orders effected continuous transformations and revitalizations in medieval Europe, but their influence was not limited to this. As they came into existence, they were ready for new tasks and new functions which the church might set for them. As the time passed, these tasks were ever-changing world wide.

The Reformation and Protestantism

The Protestant Reformation is difficult to locate with particulars. Secular historians are happy to examine the Reformation along with the Renaissance as a part of the lengthy and difficult "process of change by which the medieval world of church and empire was transformed into the modern world of nation-states and territorial churches."(32).

Roman Catholic historians have sometimes interpreted the Reformation as a "story of error and delusion, while many Protestants have viewed it as the recovery of original Christian truth and virtue."(33). It is not known for sure whether or not there are some elements of truth in these opinions.

The late H. Richard Niebuhr once made a preliminary remark that the Reformation might best be approached as a religious revolution within a social evolution. It was a remark believed to have made in a meeting of the Society for Theological Discussion in New Work city, ca. 1956 or 1957. The social revolution refers to the transformation in Europe's history from medieval to modern world; the Reformation was deeply involved in this revolution.

The inner religious revolution may be qualified or characterised by what Paul Tillich has called the "Protestant principle in the religious life of sixteenth- and seventeenth-century Europe". It should be mentioned that "Tillich defined the Protestant principle as the conviction that all human things must be held under God's judgment or criticism"(34).Conversely this means that all human things—in fact, all created beings presuppose a transcendent point of criticism. Furthermore, if human life is to find affirmative relation to God, God must take the initiative. In more traditional terms, salvation of humankind is by faith, which is in turn a gift of divine grace. H. Richard Niebuhr called this outlook radical monotheism, and asserted that as a corollary human life is placed in a state of "permanent revolution"(35). Therefore, as a result, human life under God is continuously being ruined and remade. Such is Paul Tillich's Protestant principle.

It may be mentioned here that the Reformation had its own definite applications of this principle, sometimes involving widespread modification and compromise with local forms of thinking and life style. It is also well-known that in the history of the Reformation, maters of the interior religious revolution were inseparably mixed with aspects of the outer or social revolution. "The result was the period of western history called the <u>age of the Reformation.</u>"(36).

It is widely known that this age started when on October 31, 1517, an ordinary monk called Martin Luther displayed a list of "ninety-five theses on the church door" at the German university of Wittenberg, inviting public discussion. It is widely known that The age of the Reformation ended on the continent of Europe more than a century later with the Peace of Westphalia in 1648, and in England with the Glorious Revolution of 1688. By this time people who were afraid of religious war and "fanaticism" decided to understand differences—and to pay attention to other matters. Christianity entered this age basically as one church. But eventually it resulted with five main traditions of Christianity: (1) Lutheranism, (2) Calvinism, (3) Anglicanism, (4) sectarianism, and (5) modern Roman Catholicism."(37).

The English Reformation

To begin with, the English Reformation won the support of no single renowned personality like as Luther or Calvin and was even more deeply involved in political and nationalistic affairs than the German or Swiss Reformation. It was the reaction of the English people as a separate people. "English churchmen often point to its source in an ancient tradition of English Catholic Christianity, allegedly independent of Rome."(38).

The time for "England's break with Rome was Henry VIII's (d. 1547) desire to be legally rid of his wife, Catherine of Aragon, in order that he might marry Anne Boleyn and, he hoped, "have a male heir to his throne"; still apart from these personal events were many causes. English disagreement with Rome was of long standing, going back at least to Wycliffe (d.1384). English nationalism strengthened its "muscles" in the sixteenth century. The humanism of Erasmus, Colet and More had a ready hearing in English universities and created an atmosphere of opinion bitterly critical of the church. "The writings of Luther were widely read. Incidentally, Henry VIII wrote a refutation of Luther which gained for him from the grateful people the appellation 'defender of the faith'"(39).

Henry (d. 1547) was succeeded by Edward VI (d.1553) who was in turn succeeded by his sister Mary (d. 1558) who not only persecuted the Catholics, as before, but they "were now burnt at the stake and harried from the land"(40).

England's next queen was Elizabeth (daughter of Henry). Her long reign (1558-1604) was one of England's most peaceful thus prosperous ages. In religious maters, she followed a middle way between the two "extremes of Roman Catholicism and Calvinist Protestantism". Her "Act of Supremacy of 1559 declared the Church of England to stand politically under the crown, the Book of Common Prayer to be the standard to public worship, and the episcopate and a revised Thirty-nine Articles of Religion to be the norms of the Church of England. The foundations of Anglican Christianity were laid in these decisions."(41). Commenting on the English Reformation, Hutchison remarks, "While the English Reformation produced no Luther or Calvin, nonetheless, the middle way of Anglicanism did find remarkable expression in a single book, Richard Hooker's Laws of Ecclesiastical Polity, published in 1594-1597."(42).

The Crusades

At last, it should be mentioned that in the history of religion one of the great armed conflicts was the well-known "Crusades" which proved the dynamic character of Christianity—peace is in a peaceful situation, but under an adverse situation, war must be fought for the cause of religion. However, "Papal aspiration for universal power also precipitated the Crusades", says Hans-Joachim Schoeps, "which continued for two centuries (1095-1291)."(43).

According to Christian view, as many as seven great wars were fought as a "holy war" against heretics and heathens. The main objective, according to the Papal authority, was to free the "Holy Sepulcher from the hands of the unbelievers"; but the underlying objective was to extend the power of the papacy with the conquest of the Holy Land by the Christian nations.

It should also be pointed out that many political, cultural and economic interests played important roles in the fighting of the Crusades. It is also reported that "All those preparing to give battle against the 'heathen' pinned a red cross to their shoulders, and received an indulgence for their sins."(44). Furthermore, it is stated that at the outset, the crusaders were like lawless mobs who in Germany carried out organised persecutions and massacares against the Jews. Shouting "God wills it", encouraged and inspired by powerful preachers like Pater of Amiens, the armies of the First Crusade were markedly successful. In 1099 they established the kingdom of Jerusalem headed by Duke Godfrey of Lorraine. Eventually, in 1244 Jerusalem was conquered by the Turks, who held it until 1918. However, after a period of initial zeal and courage, the Crusaders fell increasingly prey to the influences of Oriental customs and traditions.

One result of the Crusading era was the "Christian chivalric orders", which combined or merged the principles of "chivalry and asceticism". "The most important of these were the Order of Templars (1119), the Knights of St. John (circa 1120), and the Teutonic Knights (1198), who were responsible for founding the state of Prussia (circa 1250). Combat against unbelievers, protection of pilgrims, care of the sick and the wounded were the monastic and ecclesiastical tasks of these armed Knights."(45).

As for the lasting consequences of the Crusades, was the closer contact with the Muslims and their culture, the beginning of Oriental trade and commerce and widening of peoples' "intellectual horizons". As for the end result: "In spite of common ideals and actions carried out in common, the peoples of Europe emerged from the Crusades even more divided then before. Politically, the sacrifices of blood and treasure had been in vain."(46).

CH. 4: FOOTNOTES

1. Hutchison, John A., Paths of Faith, Third Edition, McGraw-Hill Book Company, Montreal, 1969, p. 358; also cf. Angus, S., Religious Quests of the Graeco-Roman World, Scribner, New York,1929.

2. Ibid., also cf. Schoeps, Hans-Joachim, The Religions of Mankind: Their Origin and Development(translated from the German by Richard and Clara Winston), Anchor Books, Doubleday & Company Inc., Garden City, New York, 1968, p. 259.

3. Cf. Scott, Ernest F., The Literature of the New Testament, Columbia, New York, 1932, pp. 21-32.

4. Mark 1:15

5. Ibid., 8: 271

6. Mathew 16: 31f.; Mark 8: 27f.; Luke 9: 18f.

7. Ibid., 26: 64; also cf. Schoeps, op. cit., p. 261.

8. Hutchison, op. cit., p. 365; also cf. Bowman, John W., The Intention of Jesus, Westminister Press, Philadelphia, 1943, pp.159ff.

9. Martin Buber, The Prophetic Faith, Macmillan, New York, 1956, pp. 179-182.

10. Hutchison, op. cit., p. 367.

11. Ibid.

12. Ibid., p. 368; also cf. Deuteronomy 6; Jeremiah 31; Hosea 11.

13. Hutchison, op. cit., p. 368.

14. Leviticus 19: 18

15. Hutchison, op. cit., p. 368.

16. Luke 10: 30-37

17. Hutchison, op. cit., p. 368 ref. Luke 12: 42-48; Luke 18: 9

18. Mathew 5: 17

19. Hutchison, op. cit., p. 369.

20. Ibid.

21. I Corinthians 15: 3-8.

22. Acts 2: 4f.; Acts 2: 41

23. Schoeps, op. cit., p. 261.

24. Ibid., p. 262.

25. Galatians, 5 and 6

26. Revelations 19: 11f.

27. Hutchison, op. cit., p. 375.

28. Ibid., p. 376.

29. Augustine, Confessions, V. 3.

30. White, L., in George Thomas (ed.),The Vitality of the Christian Tradition, Harper, New York, 1945, pp. 88f.

31. Willson Walker, A History of the Christian Church, Scribner, New York, 1959, pp. 232-238.

32. Hutchison, op. cit., p. 457.

33. Ibib.

34. Paul Tillich, The Protestant Era, University of Chicago Press, Chicago, 1948, pp. 161f.

35. H, Richard Neibuhr, The Meaning of Revelation, Macmillan, New York, 1941, p. 118.

36. Hutchison, op. cit., p. 458.

37. Ibid., also cf. Schoeps, op. cit., pp. 306ff.

38. Cf. Albert Outler's essay "The Reformation and Classical Protestantism", in George Thomas (ed.), The Vitality of Christian Tradition, Harper, New York, 1945, for a discussion of the Reformation under the first four of these topics.

39. Hutchison, op. cit., p. 467.

40. Ibid., p. 468.

41. Ibid.

42. Ibid.

43. Ibid., also cf. Schoeps, op. cit., pp. 96ff.

44. Schoeps, op. cit., p. 300.

45. Ibid., p. 301.

46. Ibid.

Ch. 5: Islam:
The Foundation Of Islamic
Religion

Islam is the third and the last of the great Semitic Religions—one of the World Religions with the Qur'an as its religious text like the Old and New Testaments and the Gospels. Like Judaism and Christianity, Islam is also a national religion with universal claims. "Mohammed [sic] the Prophet of Arabia, considered himself to be perfecting the work of Moses and Jesus, and proclaiming the newest covenant after the Old and the New Covenant"(1).

Islam is of Arab origin: Muhammad ibn 'Abdullah (577—632 C.E.), the last Prophet of Semitic religion, was born and brought up in the present day Sa'udi Arabia. As of today, there are 1. 6 billion Muslims living in 57 independent Muslim countries plus those who are living all over the world.(2).There is especially a Muslim Zone extending along the equator from Morocco in the North-West Africa through the Arab states (the last being Jordan) to Iran, Pakistan (India has 267 million Muslims), Bangladesh, and thence to Indonesia, Malaysia, Sultanate of Brunei and the Philippines, which has the vast majority of the world's Muslims. It should be mentioned here that China's north-west province, Xinxiang, is largely a Muslim province; it could be an independent Muslim country if the Muslims there have a chance to express their voice through a referendum. "The recent rise of the of the so-colled Black-Muslims in the United Sates and their convergence with traditional Islam give rise to claims that

Islam now constitutes a major American religion, having 1.5 percent of the total population. Whatever else it may be, Islam is a world religion and demands attention as such."(3).

Unlike other Semitic religions, Islam has certain fundamental principles called the Five Pillars of Islam: (1) shahada (there is no god but Allah (God) and Muhammad is His prophet; (2) salat (daily five times obligatory prayers: at dawn; at mid-day after the sun surges down the meridian; late afternoon;

in the evening—5 min. after the sunset; at night—45min. after the sunset till the dawn; (3) zakat—poor taxes—obligatory only on rich Muslims to be given to the poor Muslims only; (4) sawm (fasting in the lunar month of Ramadan obligatory for every adult Muslim men and women save some persons (the seriously ill, and for women during the monthly period (hayed, maximum seven days or according to each individual women's habit, and nifas, 40 days after a child-birth); and (5) hajj (pilgrimage to Mecca, Saudi Arabia, obligatory only on all rich Muslims—men and women; an incapable person due to physical condition, must send on his/her behalf a representative--naib to perform the hajj on his/her behalf. (A woman must be accompanied by her husband or by a person with whom her marriage is forbidden).

It may be pointed here that the Surah 112 of the Qur'an (named Al-Tawhid: "The unity) takes sharp issue with the Christian doctrine of the Trinity: "Say, He is God alone! God the Eternal He begets not and is not begotten. Nor is there like unto Him any one"! By the way, this verse is recited by the Muslims when they kiss the Black Stone of the Ka'ba after circling around the Ka'ba seven times. (The Muslim name for God, Allah, is composed of the definite article al and the ancient Semitic word for deity: Arabic ilah, Babylonian ilu; Hebrew elohim).

Pre-Islamic Arabia had many tribal cults from which Islam inherited some elements: for example, belief in jinns and iblis, spirits and devils arising out of the fierce heat of the desert. "In the series of seven heavenly messengers whom Mohammed [sic] acknowledges as his forerunners, three are Arabic"(4). Islam has inherited from the early history of the Arab tribes the "fetishistic cult of the black stone known as the Ka'ba in Mecca which was probably a meteor. The god of the sanctuary was simply called the master of the house, the God of the Ka'ba—the word meaning cube"(5).

It should be mentioned here that in addition to the fact that the Qur'an is the last of the divine revealed scripture and Muhammad is the last of the Semitic prophets, Mecca being located on the caravan trade route between Abyssinia (Ethiopia) and eastern Asia up to China, it absorbed many ideas and cultural elements from other countries. Thus a writer says, "Like all religions, Islam has been significantly influenced by its social and historical context. Indeed, like other monotheistic faiths.... Islam has affirmed and not denied or annulled the particular geographical and historical facts that lie at its base"(6). Mecca was also a well-known religious centre because of the existence of the large cube-shaped temple, "the Ka'ba, with the famous Black Stone set in the south-east corner. Pilgrims come from far on hajj, pilgrimage, "to circumambulate the temple, to kiss the Black Stone, and to worship the many icons within the temple"(7).

It may be mentioned here that the importance of the vast Muslim population all over the world, in addition to the independent Muslim countries, mentioned above, can be considered with issues ranging from oil supply (from the 15 Muslim OPEC countries (Venezuela is the 16th non-Muslim OPEC country) to world peace and stability. Here definitely is a religion which makes a difference in individual lives and in the world. Again, Toynbee has characterised the Muslim Near-East as a foil for the West.(8) In our recent times, many Muslim nations from the Arab-Middle-East to Pakistan and Indonesia have risen to challenge Western ways of politics and society. "In black regions of Africa, Islam's genuine commitment to racial equality has gained a ready hearing for this faith at precisely the time when Black Africans have come to view Christianity as a pious front for white racism."(9)

Islam, like other Semitic monotheistic religions, confesses allegiance to Allah, the One God, and leads to the rejection of other gods as false idols. Islam's expression of this principle is the idea of shirk (association of anything else with God). In other words, idolatry is totally rejected.

There is also an expression of this monotheism in the rejection of <u>Muhammadanism</u> and insistence on <u>Islam</u> as the name of this religion or faith (10). <u>Islam</u> (<u>submission</u>) to the One God, and a Muslim is one who submits. According to Muslim faith (Islam), Muhammad is a Prophet of Allah, like other Semitic prophets, mentioned above. Like other pr-Islamic monotheistic religions, Islam has Muhammad ibn 'Abdullah as its Prophet who received the Holy Book, the Qur'an, as mentioned above, the last part of the divine Book, revealed to the Semitic prophets, the first being the Torah to Moses.

The Prophet's Life

It should be stated at the outset that for a picture of Muhammad, the Qur'an is better than other documents, for it contains authentic sayings of Allah (God) and the Prophet himself. It is also a historical fact that Muhammad himself was the great builder of Islam. It bears the clearest imprint of his life and doctrines. According to historians, Muhammad ibn 'Abdullah was born in 571(11). His father had died before his birth, and his mother died when he was only six years of age. He was then taken by his grandfather, Abdul Muttalib, and after his grandfather's death, he was brought up by his uncle, Abu Talib.

One of the many stories about his early life is the one that tells that since his early life, he was very honest, sensitive, trustworthy, from which he was given the nickname <u>al-Amin</u> (the true and reliable or trustworthy one). As a young man, he was a shepherd and camel driver, making business trip first for a rich lady named Khadijah, to Yemen and Syria. He performed his duties so well and so great was their mutual liking and understanding that when he was only twenty-five, he married Khadijah, who was fifteen years his elder. That was a very happy marriage. They had five children (two sons and three daughters), of whom, only one daughter—Fatima, survived infancy.

During the year of his marriage to Khadijah, his interests in religion were maturing. Beneath the surface were developing those forces which came out in his call to be the Prophet of Islam. Seemingly, his faith in the One God extended far down, and at the same time his dislike and rejection of idolatry and his sense of an impending judgment day became profound. Obviously, it was a period of developing spiritual pressure. For several years, he used to retire for sometime to Mount Hira for lonely meditation.

Then in February 610, on the "night of Power and glory", the angel Gabriel, the messenger of Allah, "appeared, confronting his with an awe-inspiring summons". As recorded in the Qur'an, the voice said:

173

Read: In the name of they Lord who createth,

Createth man from a clot.

Read: And thy Lord is the Most Bounteous

Who teacheth by the pen,

Teacheth man that which he knew not.(12).

So was given the first revelation of the Qur'an. The angel disappeared, leaving Muhammad in distress. Then outside the cave, he heard the same voice assuring him, "O Muhammad, Thou art Allah's messenger....(13) Muhammad rushed home, shaking and feeling feverish to tell Khadijah of his experience. She put him to rest and called her cousin, Waraqa b. Nawfil, a Christian priest. He was told of Muhammad's encounter with Gabriel; he affirmed his belief, saying: "Doubtless it is the beginning of prophecy, and there shall come upon him the Great Law like as it came upon Moses."(14).

Other messages from God followed for next 22 years totaling 6,666 verses. In obedience to the divine voice which put him under orders, the Prophet began to preach, proclaiming the message he had received. A few converts were made: first was his wife, Khadijah, then his cousin, 'Ali, followed by his servants Zaid and Abu-Bakr.

As for the people of Mecca, at first they laughed at him and turned away. The scornful laughter turned to hostility as they saw in the Prophet's public speeches a threat to the popular religion and the profitable pilgrimage trade. "His uncompromising monotheism with its austere moral demands was deeply disturbing to the people of the world. Hostility took the form of persecution. Hoodlums broke up his public meetings. His followers became the victims of discrimination and attack."(15). On occasions during his Meccan period, the Prophet sent small groups of his followers to Abyssinia to escape persecution. At Mecca, the Prophet's tribe, the Hashemites, were forcibly confined to a single section of the city.

Meanwhile revelations continued to come. According to divine message, the Prophet began to preach. Many revelations have a strong sense of social justice, "and all are pervaded with a foreboding sense of doom and judgment". Here is a sample of verses of the Qur'an, revealed in Mecca:

When the sun is over thrown,
And when the stars fall,
And when the hills are moved
And when the camels big with young are abandoned,
And when the wild beasts are herded together,
And when the seas rise,

And when souls are reunited,

And when the girl child that was buried alive is asked

For what sin she was slain...

(Then) every soul will know what it hath made
ready(16).

In the meantime, according to the revelation, the Prophet
continued to preach and teach. The year 619 was an unusually
one in his life: Abu Talib died, and shortly after him, Khadijah
died. The Prophet called it "the year of suffering".

During this same year, he was also visited by a delegation
of six men from Yathrib, (a city about 300 miles to the north-west).
They waited for a man like the Prophet to go to their city to
settle their internal disputes. A delegation of twelve returned the
following year and met the Prophet at Aqaba and took an oath
to abstain from polytheism and vices and to observe the strict
discipline as the Prophet required of them. The following year,
a larger delegation of seventy-five persons came from Yathrib to
swear allegiance, confess their faith, and to urge the Prophet to
go to their city.

Tradition tells that the Meccan enemies of the Prophet
did not want to let him leave the city. There was a plot to
assassinate him, and he escaped and hid out with Abu-Bakr in a

cave on Mount Tahaur. When his enemies failed to locate him, he and Abu-Bakr left for Yathrib on a camel and made the hegira (withdraw) to Yathrib in eight days. "Thus occurred the crucial event of Muslim history. Anno Hegira 1, A.H. 1 (622 C.E.), marked the beginning of the Muslim era from which dates are still counted. "The way of Islam was launched upon the world"(17).

The problems in Yathrib were vast and complicated, but the Prophet moved decisively and with an unprecedented kind of authority which combined religious and ethical leadership with political and social leadership. He and his followers created in Yathrib (now named Medinah, the city of the Prophet), a new state and a new social order which is still regarded as the "archetypal Model" for Muslims everywhere. "Records of the Muslim community of Medinah in Qur'an and tradition have been studied by Muslims throughout their history as the model for all Muslims and all people to emulate."(18). It should be mentioned here that the Prophet's migration to Medinah marks the beginning of the Muslim calendar.

The Prophet worked upon careful consultation and full cooperation with others(19). He reformed the religious practices of the city. He erected a mosque, the first, for worship, and worked out a "cultus" and institution pleasing to Allah. "Weekly services on Friday, prayer five times daily, the call to payer (azan) from the mosque roof, prostration during prayer, alms for the poor—these and other arrangements followed in order. At first the direction in which one faced while praying (qibla) was toward Jerusalem, for the Prophet had both understanding and respect for Jewish... tradition, thinking of his movement as a fulfillment of it. He was first puzzled then incensed when the Jewish community of Medina scorned him. He broke with them openly, ordering the direction of prayer to be toward Mecca"(20). By the way, the change of the qibla from Jerusalem to Mecca was done only after the conquest of Mecca in 630 C.E.

The Prophet's gift of leadership was soon turned to external matters like foreign relations. He made many careful or sensible treaties of alliance with neighbouring peoples and also created or raised an army for Medinah. Historians point out the fundamentally defensive character of these actions, adding quotations from the Qur'an disapproving war and violence. (21).

However, not too long after his settlement in Medinah, the Prophet and his city were soon deeply involved in military expeditions. They began casually as typical raids on caravans, especially those of Mecca. However, simple operations soon increased and intensified. At the Battle of Badr, in 624, the Prophet led a band of 300 who were engaged to fight a larger

Meccan force of one thousand or more, and the Prophet and his band captured a lot of booty. The following year the Prophet and his army turned back a superior retaliatory force of Meccans. The Meccans returned in 627, and the Prophet with his army faced successfully with "trench defences", a new Persian way of defence in Arab warfare. Defending Medinah with surrounding tribes, the Prophet then moved from a position of strength to conclude a ten-year peace-treaty with Meccans. As the treaty was broken by the Meccans, the Prophet marched against Mecca, winning over minor opposition. His conquest was complete when, in 630, at the Battle of Hunayn, his army decisively defeated a coalition of tribes hostile to both Muslims and non-Muslims.

One of his first responsibilities was to perform prayer in the Ka'ba. After the "circumambulation" of the Ka'ba and kissing the Black Stone, he asked for the destruction of the many idols within and destroy completely from its walls the "painting of Abraham and others." "But the Prophet proved to be a magnanimous conqueror. His previous enemies were pardoned, and the Meccan pilgrimage was opened to all who would accept Islam. Pagan tribes within the city were given a grace period of four months to accept the new faith. If they refused, they would thereafter be subject to attack as threats to Islam. This new principle of jihad was qualified in the case of Jews and Christians."(22). Since they were people of the Book (divine Book—Torah and Injil) they had the option to keep their religion if they accepted the Muslim government and paid Jizya (a special Protection tax for non-Muslim Semitic citizens in a Muslim country). It should be mentioned here that following the conquest of Mecca, ambassadors began to come to Mecca from different neighbouring countries to acknowledge the Prophet Muhammad's sovereignty or authority over Mecca and Medinah. Many tribes of Arabia converted to Islam. "The la-ilaha illa-'llah, muhammad rasula-llah (there is no God but Allah and Mohammed is his prophet) became a battle cry for the unification of the tribes of Arabia and later for many of the nations of the Orient(23).

During the last ten years of his life, the Prophet personally commanded no fewer than twenty-seven expeditions and sent armies to thirty-eight others (65 military engagements during the last ten years of his life). Finally, he led a campaign against the Byzantine forces at the battle of Tabuk, but no clash took place.

At the end of the 10 years after the Hijra (migration to Mdina) there took place the Farewell Pilgrimage, the first pilgrimage to Mecca instituted by Muhammed himself. There the Prophet made a number of important decisions on ritual, which henceforth remained binding upon all Muslims—for example, he forbade non-believers or non-Muslims to set foot in Mecca. "He also introduced the ceremony of the hajj procession around the Ka'ba, now purified of idols, and the kissing of the black stone"(24). Not too long after, "the Prophet succumbed to mortal illness" on June 8, 632 C.E; 11 A. H.).

It was Abu-Bakr who announced to the Muslim ummah (the assembled multitude) the stunning news of the Prophet's death. Simply he declared, "O people! Lo! As for him who used to worship Muhammad, Muhammad is dead. But as for him who used to worship Allah, Allah is alive and dieth not."(25).

Fortunately, the Prophet had already laid the foundation on a solid ground for the unprecedented rapid development that made Islam the second largest religion of the world. (Christianity is the only religion, with its many divisions, that is larger than Islam). The Prophet's grave in Medinah has not become a place for worship.

Prophet Muhammad is the khatam al-anbiya, (the seal of the Prophets), or in other words, the completion of the work of Moses, David, and Jesus. He is not a mediator between Allah and man, but as the Prophet whose task it was to communicate the divine message he received through the Qur'an, to the Arabs, to begin with. His sense of mission is clearly revealed in the Qur'an, Surah 46:8: "I am not an innovator among the apostles, nor do I know what will be done with me or with you if I follow aught but what I am inspired with; nor am I aught but a plain warrior". However, later developments in the religion,---- especially under the influenced of the cult of saints in the folk religion—made the Prophet into an exemplar for believers. "Moslem mysticism made him the crown of Creation, the "perfect man"; he was even called the pre-existent light of revelation."(26). Of course, such "transfigurations" of the founder are characteristic in the history of religion. Jesus Christ is the best example in the history of religion.

Nonetheless, Prophet Muhammad may be compared with Moses: like the latter, he was the leader of a nation, a Prophet and transmitter of revelation. But the political matters in his personality and "responsibility" are far more prominent. Prophet Muhammad was successful in effectively hastening the change from "nomadism" to settled community life in Arabia, and in bringing the larger part of the population of peninsula under a "hitherto unconceivable discipline."(27).

The Message of the Qur'an Preached By the Prophet

Islam is not established on an event "but upon the Being of Allah". Islam emphasises contemplation of the divine being, which manifests as will and prescript. "The freedom of man's will depends on this ability to perceive God. Mohammed's message was initially a sermon on the judgment, a portrayal of the flames of the hell awaiting those who refused to believe. In general, eschatological notions of retribution, paradise, hell, resurrection of the dead and last judgment play a large part in Mohammedanism."(28). It is calculated that fifth of the Qur'an consists of descriptions of these last things. "Persian and Judaeo-Christian models are recognizable in many of them. The noblest title of Alllah is 'Lord of the great Judgment Day'."(29).

After the Prophet's migration to Medinah, ethical and religious matters or rule began to predominate the revelation. In addition, the Prophet also adopted some Judeo-Christian and Arab customs which were Islamised by the Prophet himself. Thus, he took over the Jewish custom of weekly congregational prayer—Sabbath—changing the day to Friday. We are also told that he included in his system the Jewish Day of Atonement, but substituted Ramadan as a month of fasting. Islam also forbids, as in the apostolic decree (Acts 15: 20), the eating of blood and the meat of animals not properly (religiously) slaughtered. In addition, Islam has forbidden (*haram*) eating of the pig or swine flesh. Islam is the only world religion which has forbidden he consumption of alcohol, save for medicine. Likewise, Islam forbids taking of interest and the games of chance that were quite common in Arabia. Circumcision, a commonly used Arab custom, was adopted by Islam even though not prescribed in the Qur'an.

Islam is a legalistic and ritualistic religion which gives great importance to observance of the law (Shari'ah) basically laid down in the Qur'an. Obedience, man's submission (aslama) to the will of God, is the basic act of freedom accepted by Islam. "Belief" in Islam means that a man fulfils his religious duties with perfection. If he does that, as the Muslims are required to do, Allah, the Almighty and All-merciful will see to the rest. "Thus Mohammed (the Prophet) reduced the relationship between God and man to an extremely simple formula."(30).

Commenting the above theory, Schoeps says, "From this there follows the Mohammedan doctrine of predestination, which in many respects is similar to Calvinistic theology. Allah guides man or leads him astray, as he [sic] wishes. Given the boundless omnipotence of God, creatures must submit in impotent dependence and utter humility. The consequence is Mohammedan fatalism. It everything is predestined by Allah, life and death, everything that happens, depends upon God's inexorable decree. Submission to kismet (fate) results in a passivity that can be dispelled only by some religious requirements, such as that of a holy war; then the passivity is transformed into fatalistic aggression."(31).

Islam does not recognise the need for sorrow in the Judeo-Christian sense. Nor do Muslims experience a real longing for salvation. Allah, being sovereign and merciful, Muslims must do all the obligations and surrender to His mercy. (Socially), this submission unites them and makes them equal in every respect. Thus Muslims regard themselves as members of a great brotherhood. Thus, in Muslim Community (ummah) there are no distinctions of race or class. At every stage of their socio-religious life, they are equal and brothers Thus, in India, Islam has broken down the caste barriers up on accepting Islam. "The simple community worship of the mosque, without pictures and without music, engenders the characteristic sense of Mohammedan brotherhood. Mohammedans are exceedingly democratic—if we except the veiled women confined in their harems and possessing few rights."(32).

Sufism :Muslim Mysticism

The Muslim ideal of equality in a simple life has continued affecting Muslim religio-communal life and eventually resulted in the formation of a special group—the mystic group. This group introduced to the Muslim Community the worship in the form of meditation and asceticism. "Sufism, one of the varieties of Mohammedan mysticism, is not the product of alien influences, but a legitimate expression of the 'monks' of the order of dervishes. Sufism acquired great influence over Islam, largely due to the work of al-Ghazali, one of the greatest theological and legal minds of all times."(33). The oldest orders of Sufis was begun in Iraq in the twelfth century. To become a Sufi means literally, to put on the woolen garment; to abandon everything that might divert one's mind from God and divine matters; and to devote oneself totally to contemplation. The first woman Sufi was Rabi'a al-Adaurya (Basri) (d. 801) of Iraq, in whom the mystical theme of the love of God found expression in such lines as the following:

> I love Thee with two loves, love of my happiness,
> And perfect love, to love Thee as is Thy due.
> My selfish love is that I do naught
> But think on Thee, excluding all beside;
> But that purest love, which is Thy due,
> Is that the veils which hide Thee fall, and I gaze on
>   Thee,
> No praise to me either this or that,
> Nay, Thine the praise for both that love and this (34).

Sufism eventually spread all over the Muslim world. Islam, being a religious- social- political system, does not permit a Muslim to abandon his full responsibility as a practicing Muslim and adopt monasticism to live in the jungle or forest. That means, if a Muslim practices Sufism and fulfills his responsibilities like all other Muslims, Islam does not prevent him, but certainly not to practice monasticism.

According to some writers' calculations, at present, about five percent of Muslims are Sufis, and they are divided into several orders and fraternities or brotherhoods. It is also estimated that more than seventy of these orders are formed by faqirs or dervishes. They, however, do not take vows of virtuous for which reason they can live a secular life. By the way, this is an example of not living a monastic life which Islam does not allow, as mentioned earlier. Their contribution to the Muslim ummah is unquestionably enormous. By a simple and popular life and preaching, they contributed enormously to the spread of Islam. It is well-known that among the dervishes (a Persian word meaning ascetics) there are some who scream, make loud cries and dance in wild scream and ecstasies; the meaning is that in this state they come near to Allah. "In some countries, the orders of dervishes are restricted or even banned nowadays; but their power is still great, especially in North Africa. The Sufis and dervishes undoubtedly made great contributions to the deepening of Mohammedan religious life—although also to veneration of saints and relics."(35).

The Five Pillars of Islam as Established by the

Qur'an:

The Five Pillars of Islam were established by the Qur'an and preached and practised by the Prophet Muhammad and his followers from the beginning of his mission. They were not established on a single occasion but rather during the Prophet's entire mission from 610 to 632 C.E. They are the fundamental duties of Muslims—men and women from the adulthood to death-- with some exceptions, as mentioned above.

(1) Shahada: (the Creed): It is obligatory for every Muslim—man and woman—to pronounce: "There is no God but Allah and Muhammad is His Prophet". "This is the sole dogmatic profession in Islam, and of the highest importance because it has preserved Islam from any inclination to deify Mohammed."(36).

(2) Salat: "canonical performance of Liturgical Worship", five times a day preceded by ablution (washing the face, two arms up to the elbows, wiping the legs up to the ankle and the head: (cf. the Q. chs.4. 43:5.6). In addition to the ablution, if some one could not use water for physical reasons or water is not available, then tayammum (wiping the face and the two arms, as it is done for ablution) must be performed with pure dust or sand before the prayer. Specific verses of the Qur'an are recited, and the movements of the body (standing, or sitting, bowing,

prostration and sitting) are prescribed in detail (Cf. "salat",
Shorter Encyclopaedia of Islam)

(3) <u>Sawum</u>: Fasting during the Arabic lunar month of
Ramadan--dawn to dusk, abstaining from food, drink and
sex—binding or obligatory upon all adult Muslim—man and
woman-- with some exceptions. "The essentially nonascetic
character of Islam is emphasized by the relaxation of these
prohibitions and the general rejoicing and festivity which take
place at night" (cf. "sawum", Shorter Encyclopaedia of Islam)

(4) <u>Zakat</u> (poor tax): The fourth Pillar is an obligatory
tax (on annual total savings of minimum ten <u>dirhams</u>, the Arab
currency) to be distributed at the end of the twelfth month of
the lunar year by all rich Muslims (man and woman) among the
poor Muslims only (first the neighbours). "Linked to almsgiving
in most formulations of Muslim faith is the wider principle of
social responsibility [sharing and caring] and social welfare which
it illustrates. The traditional operation of <u>zakat </u>has led to the
broader idea of law (<u>Shari'ah</u>) as the constitutive principle of the
Muslim community."(37).

(5) <u>Hajj</u> (The Fifth Pillar): The pilgrimage to the Ka'ba
in Mecca, Saudi Arabia, obligatory on every adult rich Muslim,
man and woman (ones on whom <u>zakat</u> is obligatory), during

the twelfth month of the lunar year, once in lifetime with some exceptions.(38). Immediately after arrival the pilgrim at Ka'ba, he/she goes to seven counterclockwise circumambulations of the Ka'ba and tries to kiss the Black Stone by touching it, only if possible to touch it, otherwise must be done symbolically. Next is to run seven times back and forth between the hills Safa and Marwa. Then pilgrims drink and splash water from the well Zamzam.

It should be mentioned that the importance of pilgrimage in preserving the vitality and unity of Islam and the Ummah (Muslim Community) is "incalculable". On his/her return home, the pilgrim is called by the "coveted" title hajji. He will be in great demand, as a guest of honour, to speak at meetings and gatherings to describe his experience. The numbers of pilgrims continue ceaselessly from not only all over the Muslim world but also from all over the world. The latest number of pilgrims is reported to be more than 2 million. This institution is an adoption of the pre-Islamic Arab custom with some necessary modifications. There are two other sacred places of pilgrimage, Medinah and Jerusalem, but they are not obligator.

Ummah :Muslim Community

At this stage, it is very important to deal with the Muslim ummah (community) which is treated by some writers as the sixth pillar of Islam for many reasons. After his migration to Yathrib (after the Prophet's migration, the Jews there changed the name to Medinah—city of the Prophet), the Prophet initiated the Charter of Medinah establishing The Ummat-ul-Medinah (Community of Medinah consisting of the Muslim migrants under the leadership of the Prophet; three Jewish tribes (Banu Nadir, Banu Qurayza and Banu Qainuqa) and the Christians were the signatories. Unfortunately, the Community did not work for long because some Madinites, especially the Jews, the richest agricultural community there, objected to the role assigned to the Prophet (a migrant) as the final judge to resolve any communal problem. After the battle of Uhud, the Prophet decided to constitute the Ummat-ul-Muslimine or Community of Muslims based on faith, brotherhood, love, caring and sharing. This battle took place against the city of Medinah in 625 in which the Jews refused to participate and defend it. Ever since the Prophet and a small group of his followers (numbering between 240—50) migrated from Mecca to Medinah in 622, the Muslims had to fight 65 wars during the last 8 years of the Prophet's life, beginning with the Battle of Badr in 624 and ending with the Battle of Tabuk in 632 C.E., 27 gozwa commanded by the Prophet himself, and the rest, 38, were sariya, the Prophet sent the Muslim army without his participation and command, without losing any save a temporary set-back at the Battle of Khandaq because of Muslims' indiscipline. Now the question is: How did it happen? The Muslims, like the non-Muslim Arabs had no special military training or weapons. The consensus of historians on this issue is that the finger-like unity, leadership and discipline helped Muslim brothers of a newly formed community to win so many military engagements. It is primarily for this reason of solidarity that the Muslim community united as brothers bound by faith, love, sharing and caring.

Commenting on the importance of the Qur'an, Schoeps says, "One of the other pillars of Islam is veneration of the Koran [sic], the inexhaustible source of edification for the believer. It is not a code of laws, like the Mishna of the Jews, since it is far from exhaustive, although the legislation of ancient Islam was based upon it. The believer regards the Koran as infallible. The Arabs imitated and surpassed the Jews' veneration of the Torah."(39).

A Brief History of Islam

Following the death of the Prophet (632 C.E.), there was a period of khilafat (Caliphate) of the four khalifa (Caliphs)—successors to the Prophet in administration matters only. Abu-Bakr, Omar, Uthman, and 'Ali, whose reigns are regarded as the "Golden Age" of the Caliphate (632-661). Following that, there began to be factional fights for political power only, which led to a break up of the ummah into sects. A constitutional dispute followed along with disagreements over interpretation of the Qur'an. The majority of the so-called Shi'ites (faction) who venerated 'Ali and his two sons—Hassan and Husayn-- as martyrs, the holders of the Caliphate and spiritual leaders, must be direct descendant of the Prophet's cousin, 'Ali. The so-called Sunnis, on the other hand, adhered to the four caliphs and later to the Umayyads in Damascus, while the so-called Shi'ites ignored the majority of the Ummah, and insisted on the Imam from the Prophet's family.

The fundamental laws, customs and institutions laid down by the Qur'an are supplemented by the sunnah--the traditional customary law. For all questions or issues, not covered by the Qur'an, Muslims turn to the acts of the Prophet, his advice and approval of others' acts as recorded by oral tradition, later compiled in the record-books known as Hadith (narratives): there are six of them (siha sitta: 1.al-Bukhari, 2. al-Muslim, (3) al-Abu-Dawud, (4) al-Tirmidhi, (5) al-Nasai and (6) al-Ibn Maja). For example, questions of the conduct of life according to the sunnah (custom) are settled by another non-canonical law of Islam called sunnah. Through these channels, a great deal of the Prophet's remarks or sayings have been handed down.

By the way, considering the social reform that the Prophet himself carried out and enforced by himself and his four successors (khalifas), breaking down the ancient tribal divisions, united the Muslim Brotherhood (Ummat-ul-Muslimin) was successfully established by the Prophet himself and maintained by his four successors (caliphs). It is really sad to read in the pages of history what happened to that united Muslim Brotherhood after the period of the khulafah-i-Rashidin (The Rightly Guided Successors of the Prophet) in 661. Reflecting on this unfortunate phenomenon of Muslim history, one writer says: "Embittered partisan struggles and the formation of rival sects marked the history of Islam soon after the death of the Prophet. The four first caliphs (Arabic khalifa, or successor), were the Koreishites: Abu-Bakr, Omar, Othman and Ali, whose reigns are regarded as the golden age of the caliphate (632-661)" (40). Following that golden period, there began bitter factional fights for power that led to a breakup of the united Muslim Community into sects. Worse, to say the least, a constitutional, or the question of order of succession raged along with dispute and disagreements over interpretation of the rule. The majority of the Shi'ites insisted that the imam must be a direct descendent of the Prophet Muhammad's cousin, 'Ali, and his son Hussayn. The "Sunnis", on the other hand, adhered to the first four Caliphs, and later to the Umayyads in Damascus, while the Shi'ites ignored the decision of the Community and insisted on the Imam from the

Prophet's family, as described befoe. "Later Shi'ite speculation held that the 'glowing bright shadow' of Mohammed was the first created principle, thereafter revealing itself in the succession of Imam."(41).

When Khalifah 'Omar ibn Khattab's army, under the green banner of Islam, conquered the Sassanid Empire (in 635 C. E.) followed by the conquest of the Eastern Byzantine Empire (Greater Syria—Syria, Iraq, Palestine and Lebanon) in 636 and Egypt in 661, thus laying the foundation of the Muslim Empire. The division between the two families('Abbasides and the Umayyads) of the Muslim Community is still alive. Ever since the descendants of the Prophet died out—the twelfth and last Imam mysteriously disappeared in 912 C. E., "the Shi'ites have waited for Allah to send a <u>Mahdi</u>, a leader of the Last Days, to bring salvation."(42).

The Shi'tes have achieved great success in Persia, making the whole country Shi'ite, and interestingly, in 1501 Shi'ism was declared the state religion of the country. It should be mentioned here that Iraq and Syria have also been Shi'ite strongholds.(43).

However, Islamic history and culture is primarily carried by the Muslims (so-called the Sunnites), which spread the rule of Islam partly by the army, partly by the Sufis, and also partly by the trader-missionaries--particularly in the Indian sub-continent (now Bangladesh, India and Pakistan) and the Far-East up to Malaysia, Indonesia and the Sultanate of Brunei, and through the whole Near-East, and Central Asia, and over North Africa to the Iberian Peninsula (Spain and Portugal) and to southern Italy—Sicily. During the seventh and eighth centuries the Caliphates of Damascus, Baghdad and Spain were set up. It is important to take note that within one hundred years after the Prophet Muhammad's death, Islamic crescent flag was hoisted on all the lands from Spain to the Caucasus, the whole Middle-East, Central Asia and Indian subcontinent. Later on, up to the Far-East, as mentioned above. "All of Europe might have fallen to them and become Mohammedan if the Franks under Charles Martel had not checked their onrush at the Battle of Tours" [and Portier] in 732(44).

Let us conclude the present subject by citing the words of Schoeps who brings the history of Islamic power to an end with these words: "Although the central power of the Caliphate declined from the tenth century on, Islam continued to gain ground. From Gibraltar to the Himalayas the green flag of the Prophet waved for centuries. The Balkans, too, fell entirely into the hands of the Moslems. In 1453 Byzantium was conquered, and the Osmans planted the crescent upon Hagia Sophia. In 1529 the victorious armies of Moslems stood before the gates of

Vienna; it was not until the naval battle of Lepanto in 1571 and the battle on the Kahlenberg before the walls of Vienna in 1685 that the 'Turkish peril' was at last banished. Between the eleventh and the sixteenth centuries northern India and Indonesia were also conquered by Islam. But gradually the secular power of the Mohammedans began to fade. Islam, internally disunited, lacked centralistic leadership."(45).

The Present Situation

Presently Islam has spread all over the world with an estimated total population of over 1.6 billion Muslims. There are 57 independent Muslim countries throughout Asia especially in Central Asia. In the Far East, Indonesia is the largest Muslim country with a population of over of 250 million people, its industrial prosperity is unparallel in the Muslim world; one of the 16 oil producing countries (a member of OPEC: there are 15 Muslim OPEC countries of which Saudi Arabia number one and Iran number six followed by Iraq and all the Persian Gulf countries; in the continent of Africa, the Sudan, Senegal and all the north-western Mediterranean coastal Muslim countries are also oil-producing nations). Bangladesh and Pakistan two other heavily populated Muslim countries (each has over 200 million people). India, a Hindu majority country, is said to have as many as 264 million Muslims. Muslim missionaries have been very successful in converting outcastes or low-castes especially from India and the Black people of Central and South Africa. Commenting on the present situation almost all over the world and the spread of the message of Islam, one writer says: "Today the power of technological civilization and industrialization is presenting Islam with wholly new problems. So also is the awakening nationalism among the African and Asiatic peoples, since religion and the state no longer simply coincide even in the Orient. Serious social tensions are coming to the fore; the monopoly of land by wealthy sheiks is no longer tamely accepted everywhere in the Mohammedan world. The Koran [sic] is frequently hailed as an 'anti-capitalistic book'. There are strong movements, seeking adaptation of Islam to the modern world without relinquishing the core of the old doctrines and traditions. A good deal of agitation for reform now proceeds from the principal seat of Islamic scholarship, the thousand-year-old El-Azhar Mosque in Cairo, ..."(46).

Changes to the legal position of women, and civil legislation on the European model as far as the government could go, has been carefully carried out in Turkey, Egypt and to some degree in Iran. The greatest of all Muslim reformers was the famous military general-reformer, Mustafa Kamal Ataturk (1881-1938) who carried out a drastic reform: following the First World War he abolished the Caliphate, thus separating religion and state. He also replaced the original Arabic language with the Roman alphabet and issued a decree that the Turkish language be used in prayer so that those who pray could understand the language of their prayer. Later, however, this extreme or drastic laicism or secularism was somewhat softened; religious institutions along with the Arabic language were reintroduced into mosques and state schools. In Iran, also, the influence of the <u>moftis</u> (the interpreters of religious law and those who are allowed to issue verdict in a controversial matters) and all other 'ulama (religious scholars) are once more on the increase.

Speaking about the religious reforms in Islam, Schoeps says: "The principal religious reform movement, puritanical and ascetic in nature, was that of the Wahabis, which started in the eighteenth century, its last uncontested leader was King Ibn Saud, who died in 1953. The Wahhabis wanted to restore the original purity of ancient Islam, and therefore rejected all innovations, such as celebration of the Prophet's birthday, and the cult of saints, tombs and relics. Using strict military discipline, they waged a campaign against superstition and the cult of demons, with the result that Saudi Arabia was able to enter the modern age."(47).

It should be stated clearly that the syncretistic school groups have gone further away from the original or fundamental doctrines of Islam. Among these are the Bahai sect, a branch of Shi'ism, "which attempts to unite all religions on a pacifistic, humanitarian basis". It was founded in 1950s by Bahaullah (God's radiance). There is also the Ahmadia group in the Indian subcontinent (now Bangladesh, India and Pakistan) since 1880, which holds rationalistic thus modernistic views and carries on missionary activities in both Europe and North America. The Agakhanies are another branch of Shi'ism.

The author, Hans-Joachim Schoeps concludes in his book the section: 'The Religion of Islam' with these words: "In fifty-two nations, the doctrines of the Prophet have won a firm hold over the overwhelming majority of the people"(48). In other words, today Islam is a growing faith that is spreading all over the glove and is embraced by diverse peoples, as stated above. That this number is likely to increase there is no doubt.

CH. 5: ISLAM: FOOTNOTES

1. Schoeps, Hans-Joachim, <u>The Religions of Mankind: Their Origin and Development,</u> (translated from the German by Richard and Clara Winston), Anchor Books, Doubleday & Company, Inc., Garden City, New York, 1968, p. 242.

2. Cf. Hedayetullah, Muhammad, <u>Dynamics of Islam</u>: <u>An Exposition,   Trafford,</u>Victoria,B.C.,Canada,   2002,   pp. 210-215 and notes 72-79.

3. Kenneth Morgan (ed.), <u>Islam—The Straight Path</u>, Ronald, New York, 1958, pp. 184f.

4. Schoeps, <u>op. cit.</u>, p. 243.

5. <u>Ibid</u>.

6. Hutchison, John A., <u>Paths of Faith</u>, Third Edition, McGraw-Hill Book Company, Montreal,

7. 1969, p.394.

8. <u>Ibid</u>., p. 395.

9. <u>Ibid</u>. For more information about Mecca an important religious centre especially for

10. pilgrimage, cf. p. 396; Toynbee, A., <u>Civilization on Trial</u>, Oxford University Press, Fair

11. Lawn, N. J., 1948, pp.184f.

12. Hutchison, op. cit., p.394.

13. Gibb,H. A. R., Mohammedanism, Mentor Books, New American Libra, New AYork, 1955.

14. Morgan op. cit., p. 6.

15. Qur'an, XCV1, 1-5, in The Meaning of the Glorious Koran, Mohammed Marmaduk

16. Pickthall(traans.), Mentor Books, New American Library, New York, 1953, p. 445.

17. Sir William Muir, Life of Mahomet, Smith Elder, London, 1878, p. 132; also cf. Schoeps, op. cit., pp. 244f.

18. .Hutchison, op. cit., p. 397.

19. Quran, LXXX1, 1—4 in The Meaning of the Glorius Koran, op. cit., p. 431.

20. Hutchison, op. cit., p. 399.

21. Ibid.

22. Mogran, op. cit., p. 14.

23. Hutchison, op. cit., p. 399.

24. Morgan, op. cit., p. 14.

25. Hutchison, op. cit., p. 400.

26. Schoeps. op. cit., p. 247.

27. .bid.

28. The Meaning of the Glorious Koran, op. cit., p. xxv 11.

29. Schoeps, op. cit., p. 249.

30. .Ibid.

31. Ibid., p.250.

32. Ibid.;

33. Schoeps, op. cit. 252; also cf. Hutchison, op.cit., pp. 415f

34. Quoted in Gibb, op. cit., p. 103 (ref. Nicholson, p., Literary History of the Arabs, p. 234).

35. Schoeps, op. cit., p. 252.

36. Ibid., p. 253.

37. Hutchison, op. cit., p. 407; also cf. "Zakat", Shorter Encyclopaedia of Islam.

38. Hutchison, op. cit., p. 407; also cf. "Hajj", Shorter Encyclopaedia of Islam.

39. Schoeps, op. cit., p. 253.

40. Ibid., p. 254.

41. Ibid., p. 255.

42. Ibid.

43. Ibid. It should be pointed out here that the Shi'ites are divided into many sects or branches: such as the Druses, the Nasiris and the Ism'ilis of whose Indian branch was headed by the well-knwn Aga Khan, the forty-ninth Imam; at present his son is the imam.

44. Ibid., p. 256.

45. Ibid.

46. Ibid., p. 257.

47. Ibid.

CONCLUSION

The study of the world's living religions has made it abundantly clear that all religions of the world are fundamentally the same—devotion to the Ultimate Reality in different ways. Practicing a religion, no matter the way it is done, is human nature, and to find an object, seen or unseen, is a matter of personal as well as national concern. For instance, Indian religion, Hinduism, the oldest in the world, is not a revealed religion, rather it is a phenomenon of the sages who spent long times in unpopulated areas like forests, and through these devotions, they developed some mystical ideas during the period of 1500 to 1000 B.C., which constituted the basis of Hinduism as it is described in the Vedas—the ultimate Reality is Brahman. During the long course of its development, Hinduism also developed the idea of a trinity—Brahma, Vishnu and Shiva. It is also known that the Vedas subsequently developed what is called the idea of monism.

Of the Hindu religious literatures, the <u>Upanishads</u> is significant for it contains the mystical aspect of Hinduism vividly, and its dominant theme is the "absolute reality". It should be stated clearly that the goal of Hinduism is <u>nirvana</u>. That is, to realize the existence of an Ultimate Reality (Vagavan--God).

Sikhism is a by-product of Kabir: The Apostle of Hindu-Muslim unity. It is a Sufistic religion believing in Ultimate Reality. Because of its uncompromising ambition for independence, it came in conflict with the Mughal government. Having lost the political ambition, the Sikhs turned their attention to religious and communal matters such as the communal meal and Sikh's ethics from quietism to activism. Since the Sikhs came from different Hindu castes, they formed the casteless community of the Khalsa. Politically, this community eventually turned to a fighting theocracy. Religiously, Sikhism is a monotheistic system as it is vividly clear from the Sikh religious literature—Adigranth. This unity took shape after diversity.

In Buddhism, Buddha was a mystic-philosopher believing in salvation. His dissatisfaction with the worldly life led him to seek salvation—to go to Ultimate Reality, not mentioned though.

However, later Buddhism developed the idea of an Ultimate Reality.

In Jainism Mohavira believed in "tirthankara", one of the 23 tirthankaras, but believed in emancipation (<u>moksha</u>). Jainism also believed in the existence of a super power, also believed in the separation from this world—going to the sphere of bliss. This is an indirect admission of the ultimate goal. Jainas believed in gods—a kind of diversity in the belief of god.

When we study Zoroastrianism, we find a kind of divine book—Bible Avesta, a simple monotheistic religion. Zoroaster considered himself a prophet and believed in one god--Ahura Mazda. From this unity, we find the diversity in later Zoroastrianism which developed the principle of moral and cosmic dualism, and Zoroaster himself was deified. However, it believed in universal salvation.

When we turn our attention to the Chinese religion, we find the development of Mahayana Buddhism which developed the doctrine of Bodhisatva. Of the ten Buddhist sects, Buddhism of the "School of the Pure Land" and the "School of Meditation" were very successful. The "School of the Pure Land" became a religion of personal salvation which is sought in the heavenly Buddha's paradise. The supreme Buddha—Buddha Amitabha is shown in different temples as majestic and kind.

Buddhism of the "School of the Pure Land" also eventually became a religion of grace. It is abundantly clear that this religion is an example of diversity in religious concepts, for it talks of heaven and salvation after death.

It may be mentioned here that the notable religious figures of ancient China were Confucius and Laotzu whose main idea was <u>ultimate concern of Valuation.</u> There are eight major themes in the teaching of Confucius, the most important is Li.

In the case of the Japanese Buddhism, there is a new theme. It is inclined to absorb the ways of the natives and to enter into an alliance with their religion—Shintoism. Buddhism did not fully merge with Shintoism even though it adopted some elements from the latter such as sooth-saying and the sale of amulets. Later it adopted Shintoism's "Sectarianism". Shintoism was and still a very liberal system as a result it adopted as much as transmitted from language and art to virtually all significant elements of the society. By the way, Japanese Buddhism is as much Japanese as Buddhist. An important example of diversity in religious life.

Finally, Shintoism (Path of the gods or Way of the Sublime) is a national religion of Japan without a founder and a dogmatic scriptures being a practical religion concerning matters of this world, focusing only on family and national matter. Another clear example of diverse religion.

The three Semitic religions, namely, Judaism, Christianity and Islam are well-known monotheistic religions, the best examples of unity in this respect. However, with the passage of time, they developed diversity. It is well-known that Israel did not have a monotheistic religion at the earliest stage because the Hebrews acknowledged other deities, though they tried to worship only One God, Jahveh. It is also well-known that Israel did not practise a monotheistic religion until the time of prophet Deutero Isaiah.

With the passing of the time, the Israelites developed divisions in their religious and cultural life which resulted in the divisions known as orthodox, conservative and modern Jews who live their respective lives. This is another clear example of unity and diversity in religion. Further- more, Judaism also represents a careful amalgamation of religious and national life. Finally, with the passage of time, Judaism too developed mysticism which is quite different from the orthodox religion.

When we examine the religious life of the Christians, we find that the present-day Christ- ianity is not what was founded by the early Christians who established this religion on the "blood" of Jesus Christ. At the beginning, it was a united system but through the ages, there developed as many as 12 divisions including a philosophical Christianity. It is commonly held that Christianity is the best example of sectarian pattern. Sectarian pattern developed during the age of the Reformation. It should be noted that sectarian ideas and activities appeared in England as well as in on the continent of Europe during the sixteenth and seventeenth centuries. Some spoke of the Christian diversity like a pyramidal structure on the top of which the Pope is sitting.

When we study the history of Islam, it becomes clear that during the later development, Islam is divided into two main factions—Sunni and Shi'a. In the latter division, there had been further divisions—as many as twelve. Thus the present-day Islam is not the one united system, rather divided, thus a diversified system of religion. However, like other Semitic religions, mentioned above, Islam remained united as far as the Ultimate Reality is concerned.

It should be mentioned that a farther diversity in Islam happened when Sufism (mysticism) began to appear in the society beginning from the time of Rabi'a al-Adaurya (also known as Basri d. 801 C. E.).It is also known that against the strict monotheism of the Islamic tradition, mysticism placed the immediacy of God's presence in their hearts—as in the Qur'an says: "nearer than one's jugular vein".

Thus, from the earliest times of humanity's existence, we can see there has been a universal quest for meaning and answers to fundamental questions such as, "What is our place in the universe?" "What is the ultimate goal or purpose of our lives?" "How should we live and conduct ourselves?" and so forth. Each religion purports to give answers to these questions and to design a path for the devotees to follow. Underlying the diverse faiths, we can discern a common thread that eventually connects them at some level---the belief that the final goal is union with the Ultimate Reality which is most often associated with Compassion, Love, and Mercy.

BIBLIOGRAPHY

Albright, William F. From the Stone Age to Christianity. Anchor
Books, Doubleday, Garden City, N. Y. 1957.

Allchi, B. and Allchi R. The Birth of Indian Civilization. Penguin,
Baltimore, 1968.

Anderson, B. Understanding the Old Testament. Prentice Hall,
Englewood-Cliffs, N. J. 1957.

Angus, S. Religious Quests of the Greco-Roman World, Scribner,
New York, 1953.

A. Pegis (ed.). Introduction to St. Thomas Aquinas. Modern
Library, New York, 1948.

Arberry, A. The Doctrine of the Sufis. Cambridge, London,
1935.

Arnold, T. and Guillaume, A. The Legacy of Islam. Clarendon
Press, Oxford, 1931.

Arther Jeffrey (ed.). Islam: Muhammad and His Religion. Liberal Arts, New York, 1958.

Barodia, V. C. History and Literature of Jainism, Bombay, 1907.

Basham, A. L. The Wonder That was India. Grove Press, New York, 1959.

Benedict, R. Patterns of Culture. Mentor Books, New York, 1946.

Bettenson, H. Documents of the Christian Church. Oxford University Press, Fairlawn, N. J.1947.

Betts, J. D. (ed.). Phenomenology of Religion. Harper & Row, New York, 1969.

Boradia, V. C. History and Literature of Jainism. Bombay, 1907.

Bornkamm, G. Jesus of Nazareth. Harper, New York, 1960.

Brown, R. The Spirit of Protestantism. Oxford University Press, London, 1961.

Butt, E. A. Man Seeks the Divine. Harper & Row, New York, 1964.

Chan, W. T. The Way of LaoTzu. Liberal Arts, New York, 1963.

Chen, K. Buddhism in China. Princeton, Princeton, N. J., 1964.

Danielou, A. Hindu Polytheism. Bollingen Series, Pantheon Books, New York, 1964.

de Bary, William T. (ed.). Sources of the Japanese Religion. Columbia, New York, 1958.

Dawson, C. Religion and the Rise of Western Culture. Image Books, Doubleday, 1958.

Dawson, H. C. Religion and Culture. Maridian Books, New York, 1947.

Dhalla, M. N. History of Zoroastrianism. Oxford University Press, London, 1938.

Durkheim, E. Elementary Forms of the Religious Life. Free Press, New York, 1965.

Eliade, M. Patterns in Comparative Religion. Sheed, New York, 1959.

Eliot, Sir Charles. Hinduism and Buddhism. Routledge, London, 1954.

Feuerbach, L. The Essence of Christianity. Harper, New York, 1957.

Gibb, H. A. R. Mohammedanism. Mentor Books, New American Library, New York, 1955.

,, ,, Modern Trends in Islam. University of Chicago Press, Chicago, 1947.

Goldziher, I. Mohammed and Islam. Yale, New Haven, Conn, 1917.

Guillaume, A. Life of Mohammed. Oxford University Press, London, 1955.

H. Jacobi (tr.). "Jaina Sutras": <u>Sacred Books of the East</u>. XII, Oxford University Press, London, 1884.

Herberg, W. <u>Protestant, Catholic, Jew</u>. Anchor Books, Doubleday, Garden City, N. Y. 1960.

Hitti, Philip K. <u>The Arabs</u>. Regency, Chicago, 1956.

Hocking, W. F. <u>Living Religions and a World Faith</u>. Harper, New York, 1940.

Holton, Daniel C. <u>The National Faith of Japan: A Study in Modern Shinto</u>, Dulton, New York, 1938.

Hopkins, T. <u>The Hindu Religious Tradition</u>. Dickenson, Belmont, Calif.,1971.

Iqbal, M. <u>Reconstruction of Religious Thought in Islam</u>. Oxford University Press, London, 1934; Harvard, Cambridge, Mass., 1947.

James, E. O. <u>History of Religion</u>. Harper, New York, 1957.

James, W. <u>The Varieties of Religious Experience</u>. Longmans, London, 1902.

K. Morgan(ed.). <u>The Path of the Buddha</u>. Ronald, New York, 1956.

Keith, Arther B. <u>The Religion and Philosophy of the Vedas and the Upanishads. I,</u> Harvard, Cambridge, Mass, 1925.

Kenneth Morgan (ed.). <u>The Path of the Buddha</u>. Ronald, New York, 1950.

,, ,, ,, <u>Islam—The Straight Path</u>. Ronald, New York, 1958.

Kenneth W. Morgan (ed.). The Religion of the Hindus. Ronald, New York, 1953.

King, W. L. Introduction to Religion. Harper, New York, 1954.

Kitagawa, J. Religion in Japanese History.Columbia, New York, 1966.

Knox, John. Jesus: Lord and Christ. Harper, New York,1958.

Lang, A. The Making of Religion. Longmans, London, 1998.

Lienhardt, G. Divinity and Experience. Clarenton Press, Oxford, 1965.

Lynn White in George Thomas (ed.). The Vitality of the Christian Tradition. Harper, New York, 1945.

MacDonell, A. A. A Vedic Reader for Students. Oxford University Press, London, 1953.

Malinowski, B. Magic, Science and Religion. Doubleday, Garden City, N. Y. 1965.

,, ,, The Foundations of Faith and Morals. Oxford, 1936.

Marett, R. R. The Threshold of Religion. Oxford,1936.

Marshall, et al., J. Mohenjodaro and the Indus Vally Civilization. Oxford University Press, London,1931.

Martindale, C. C. The Faith of the Roman Church. Sheed, New York, 1950.

McGiffert, A. A History of Chriatian Thought. Scribner, New York, 1933.

Moore, G. F. **Birth and Growth of Religion,** Scribner, New York, 1927.

,, ,, ,, History of Religions. I, New York,1948.

Muir, Sir William. Life of Mahomet. Smith Elder, London, 1878.

Murti, T. P. V. The Central Philosophy of Buddhism. G. Allen, London, 1955; Nebraska Press, Lincoln, 1960.

Needham, J.(ed.). **Science, Religion and Reality, Macmillan, New York, 1925.**

Niebuhr, H. R. **The Meaning of Revelation. Macmillan, New York, 1948.**

,, ,, ,, Redical Monotheism and Western Culture. Harper, New York, 1943.

,, ,, **The Protestant Era. University of Chicago, 1948.**

Noss, J. B. **Man's Religion,** 2nd. **ed., Macmillan, New York, 1955.**

Otto, R. **The Idea of the Holy. Oxford University Press, London, 1923.**

Parrinder, G. **Worship in the World's Religions, Faber, London, 1961.**

Pickthal,Mohamed Marmaduk (trns.). The Meaning of the Glorious Koran. Mentor Books, New American Library, New York, 1953.

Pratt, J. B. India and its Faiths. Houghton Mifflin, Boston, 1915.

,, ,, The Pilgrimage of Buddhism. Macmillan, New York, 1928.

Pritchard, J. B. <u>Ancient Near Eastern Texts</u>. Princeton, Princeton, N. J. 1955.

R. Ferm (ed.). <u>Readings in the History of Christian Thought</u>. Holt, New York 1964.

Radhakrishnan, S. <u>The Principal Upanishads.</u> Harper, New York, 1953.

Robinson, H. W. <u>Inspiration and Revelation in the Old Testament</u>. Oxford University Press, London, 1946.

Ross, F. <u>Shinto</u>: <u>The Way of Japan</u>. Beacon Press, Boston, 1965.

Schmidit, W. <u>The Origin and Growth of Religion</u>. Dial, New York, 1931.

Schweitzer, A. <u>The Quest of the Historical Jesus</u>. A. & C. Black, London, 1936.

Singh, Khushwant. <u>The Sikh Today</u>. Orient Lougmans, Calcutta, 1964.

Smart, N. <u>The Religious Experience of Mankind</u>. Scribner, New York, 1969.

Smith, W. C. <u>The Meaning and End of Religion.</u> Macmilan, New York, 1963.

,, ,, ,, <u>Islam in Modern History</u>. Mentor Books, New York, 1956.

Stace, W. T. <u>The Teachings of the Mystics</u>. Mentor Books, New American Library, New York, 1060.

Streng, F. <u>Understanding Religious Man.</u> Dickenson, Belmont, California, 1969.

Suzuki, D. T. Zen Buddhism. William Barrett (ed.), Anchor Books, Doubleday, Garden City, N.Y.,1956.

Thompson, L. Chinese Religion. Dickenson, Belmont, Calif., 1969.

Tillich, P. The Protestant Era. University of Chicgo Press, Chicago, 1948.

Van der Leeuw, G. Religion in Essence and Menifestation. Harper & Row, New York, 1963.

Von Grunebaum, G. Modern Islam. University of California Press, Barkeley, 1955.

Von Rod, G. The Message of the Prophets. SCM Press, London, 1965.

W. Lessa, and E.Vogt, Reader in Comparative Religion, Harper & Row, New York, 1972.

Wach, J. Sociology of Religion. Chicago University Press, Chicago, 1944.

Walker, W. A History of the Christian Church. Rev. ed., Scriber, New York, 1959.

Ware, James R. The Sayings of Confucius. Mentor Books, New American Library, New York, 1971.

Watt, W. M. Muhammad: Prophet and Statesman. Oxford University Press, London, 1961.

William T. de Bary (ed.). Sources of Indian Tradition. Columbia, New York, 1958.

William T. de Bary et al. (eds.). Sources of the Chinese Tradition. Columbia, New York, 1960.

Wolfson, Hanry A. Philo: Foundations of Religious Philosophy of Judaism, Christianity, and **Islam. Harvard. Cambridge, Mass., 1947.**

Zaehner, R. C.(ed.). Concise Encyclopedia of Living Faiths. Hawthorn, New York, 1951.

,, ,, ,,The Dawn and Twilight of Zoroastrianism. Putnam, New York, 1961.

Zimmer, H. Philosophies of India. Meridian Books, New York, 1957.